LA Tribune Publishing

The Right of Muriel Blanc to be identified as the
Author of the work has been asserted by her in accordance
with the Copyright Act 1988.

LA Tribune Publishing
name has been established by LA Tribune.

All Rights Reserved.

No part of this publication may be reproduced, distributed, or transmitted in any form or by any means, including photocopying, recording, or other electronic or mechanical methods without the prior and express written permission of the author or publisher, except in the case of brief quotations embodied in critical reviews and certain other noncommercial uses permitted by copyright law.

Printed in the United States of America
ISBN- 9781088082652
Library of Congress Control Number: 2023947652
Copyright@2023 Muriel Blanc

To Tom,
Thank you for your teaching and wisdom. Much Gratitude
Muriel

Awakening the Soul's Vibration

Sacred Mandalas for Healing and Transformation

By
Muriel Blanc

DEDICATION

"Committed to all those on the journey of inner healing and transformation.

In the symphony of existence, keep in mind: 'Deep within your soul resides an endless source of healing. Embrace it, and you'll discover the limitless strength to mend your spirit.'"

Let these mandalas be your companions on the path to self-discovery, offering insights, healing, and profound transformation with every glance. In their intricate patterns, you'll find the keys to unlocking your highest potential. Just take a few slow breaths and let the magic unfold.

- Muriel

ABOUT THE AUTHOR

For the past 30 years, Muriel has been a beacon of hope and a catalyst for profound change in the lives of countless individuals. With an innate gift of possessing a deep understanding of alchemy and the 12 universal laws and an unwavering commitment to their well-being, she has facilitated their journeys towards unlocking their true selves, igniting the flames of their full potential, and manifesting lives rich in abundance, love, and well-being. Her impact on those she touches is nothing short of extraordinary, earning her a reputation as a "gifted healer and coach," a "guiding light," and a force of "nature."

With an alchemical blend of compassion, empathy, and intuition, Muriel creates a safe, nurturing space where individuals can explore their self-limiting beliefs. These deeply ingrained patterns of thinking often restrict personal growth and fulfillment. In this sacred space, Muriel empowers her clients to challenge and replace the beliefs with ones that align with their true goals and aspirations. Her toolkit is diverse and powerful, drawing from an array of transformational healing modalities such as Energetic Inner Child work, shamanic practices, reiki, sound healing, and color therapy.

Muriel's intuitive connection with her clients is a profound gift. She delves into the depths of their souls, illuminating hidden patterns that have been blocking their progress. Vulnerability becomes strength in her presence, as clients courageously confront their fears and insecurities, ultimately emerging with newfound clarity and purpose.

In her artistic expression, Muriel crafts custom Mandalas imbued with sacred geometry based on each client's Divine Soul Blueprint. These Mandalas serve as powerful talismans, resonating with transformation and alignment, visual representations of the alchemical journey.

Through these transformative techniques, Muriel helps her clients recalibrate their emotional, mental, physical, and energy bodies. The outcomes are awe-inspiring: self-love blooms where doubt once resided, acceptance replaces self-criticism, trust in the benevolence of the universe takes root, and the need for control surrenders to an embrace of life's unfolding journey.

At the core of Muriel's mission is a simple yet profound belief: that every individual is inherently whole and complete, an integral thread in the fabric of the universe. She is unwavering in her commitment to nurturing this belief within her clients, guiding them to trust their own internal compass, and empowering them to pursue their dreams with unwavering faith.

Muriel invites those ready for profound change to embrace the transformative power of her coaching and healing. Together, they unlock the latent potential within, transmuting life's challenges into the purest gold of self-realization, joy, and fulfillment.

TABLE OF CONTENTS

Dedication		iv
About The Author		v
Chapter 1:	Introduction to Sacred Mandalas	1
Chapter 2:	Exploring the Soul's Vibration	15
Chapter 3:	Healing Through Mandalas	29
Chapter 4:	Creating Sacred Mandalas	37
Chapter 5:	Sacred Mandalas for Transformation	63
Chapter 6:	Integrating Sacred Mandalas into Daily Life	91
Chapter 7:	Sharing the Healing Power of Mandalas	101
Chapter 8:	Nurturing the Soul's Vibration	117
Conclusion:	Embracing the Soul's Vibration through Sacred Mandalas	123

Chapter 1

Introduction to Sacred Mandalas

Understanding the Power of Sacred Mandalas

Understanding the Power of Sacred Mandalas

In this book, I share my personal experience and the knowledge that I gained when I visited the temple of the goddess Hathor in Egypt in January 2020. As an explorer of ancient wisdom and a student of sacred geometry, I was struck by the powerful energy and rich symbolism of the intricate design, vibrant colors, and the many symbolisms that I encountered at the temple.

For many years, I have been interested in the power of sacred geometry and its role in spiritual growth and self-discovery. When I visited the temple of Hathor, I knew that I was in a special place and that I was meant to be there.

During my visit, I felt a sense of gratitude and reverence wash over me, and I knew that I was in the presence of something truly sacred. Upon my return to the United States, I was compelled to put the many messages I was receiving on canvas, and different Mandalas and sacred geometry started to take shape. I then offered my clients custom Mandalas based on their soul blueprint and vibration as meditative healing tools. After receiving their mandalas, many reported a sense of peace and inner healing. I have added some of the testimonials I received at the end of this book.

Personally, I have found mandalas to be an invaluable aid in my self-discovery and a deeper understanding of the divine. During my meditations, they help me focus and allow me to reach a place of deeper connection with the cosmos and my own soul.

In our quest for healing and transformation, we often overlook the profound impact that sacred mandalas can have on our journey. These intricate and vibrant geometric patterns hold within them a power that goes far beyond their aesthetic appeal. They possess the ability to awaken our soul's vibration and guide us toward a state of holistic well-being.

For those in need of healing and yearning to follow their soul's vibration, sacred mandalas offer a unique pathway. These ancient symbols have been revered by cultures across the globe for centuries, for their ability to connect us with our inner selves and the divine energy that surrounds us. By engaging with these sacred patterns, we can tap into a wellspring of healing energy that exists within us.

A sacred mandala is not merely a beautiful piece of art; it is a portal to the depths of our souls. Through its intricate design and harmonious colors, it creates a sacred space where we can explore our innermost emotions, fears, and desires. As we gaze upon a sacred mandala, we are invited to delve deep into our subconscious, allowing us to unlock hidden aspects of ourselves and release any emotional blockages that hinder our healing process.

The healing journey that a sacred mandala offers is a holistic one, encompassing our physical, emotional, and spiritual well-being. As we immerse ourselves in its intricate patterns, we begin to align our chakras, balance our energy centers, and restore harmony within ourselves. The power of these mandalas lies in their ability to activate the body's natural healing mechanisms, allowing us to experience profound physical and emotional transformation.

Moreover, sacred mandalas act as a bridge between our conscious and unconscious minds. They serve as a visual representation of the interconnections of all things and remind us of our inherent unity with the universe. By contemplating a mandala, we can gain a deeper understanding of our place in the grand tapestry of existence, fostering a sense of purpose, meaning, and connection.

For those seeking healing and looking to follow their soul's vibration, sacred mandalas offer a transformative journey like no other. They have the power to awaken our soul's vibration, heal our physical and emotional wounds, and guide us toward a state of holistic well-being. By engaging with these sacred symbols, we open ourselves up to a world of possibilities, where healing and transformation become not just a destination, but also a lifelong journey.

History and Origins of Mandalas

History and Origins of Mandalas

For centuries, people from around the world have been fascinated and inspired by the Mandalas' beauty and meaning as well as their complex forms. The word Mandala derives its name from the Sanskrit term for "round" or "complete," and can serve as a portal to one's own subconscious.

Mandalas can also be identified quite often by the term Sacred Geometry and are found everywhere in nature, the cosmos, and within our own bodies. How is this possible? Take the time out of your busy schedule to look at the celestial objects or luminary which are the moon, and the sun, in a shape of a circle, in nature look within the trees, plants, and flowers, they have a perfect circle or a perfect geometric pattern, in the human body, our blood cells, our pupils are circular. No wonder, why one can find wonder and magic in looking at a mandala.

The Mandala's intricate, circular designs have a rich history and cultural significance that spans many different traditions and periods. One of the key characteristics of mandalas is their geometric shapes emanating from a central point and their different colors. In some traditions, some specific colors relate to divinities or different aspects of the universe.

They can take many different styles, from simple circles, triangles, squares, and diamonds to elaborate, multi-layered shapes that combine symbols and imagery. Some mandalas are purely decorative, while others are filled with deep spiritual meaning, a certain vibration, and frequency, and used as tools for meditation, self-exploration, and healing.

The art of mandalas is found in many religions and cultures around the world, resulting in a long and rich history for them. Mandalas are frequently included in the construction and architecture of temples, churches, and cathedrals.

The following is a small attempt to explain the development of mandalas over the course of history and their cultural significance and in some instances how mandalas are utilized in these contexts:

Mandalas may be displayed in the stained-glass windows or in the mosaic tile work on the floors and walls of Christian cathedrals. In this setting, mandalas can be viewed as a means of depicting the journey of the soul or of establishing a connection with the divine.

- Mandalas are utilized in the religion of Hinduism as a graphic representation of the cosmos and the repetitive patterns that

make up life. As a means of establishing a connection with the divine during rites and ceremonies, they frequently show deities, the abodes where they reside, and various other cosmic symbols.
- Buddhist temples: Mandalas are frequently utilized in Buddhist temples as a means of illustrating the spiritual path and of establishing a connection with the divine. Mandalas can be included in the design of the temple's construction, or they might serve as a focal point for meditative and devotional practices.
- In Buddhism, mandalas serve a similar purpose, acting both as a visual depiction of the order of the cosmos and as a tool for attaining enlightenment. Mandalas can depict the palace of a god, with each level standing for a distinct stage of spiritual development or accomplishment.

  It is common practice in Tibetan Buddhism to construct elaborate mandalas out of colored sand as a part of elaborate ceremonies. After the ceremony, the mandalas are ritually destroyed to represent the transience of all things.
- Mandalas can be produced in Native American traditions as a part of healing ceremonies or as a method to recognize and connect with the natural world. These are both examples of ways that mandalas can be used.
- Celtic mandalas, on the other hand, are deeply rooted in the mystical traditions of ancient Ireland and Scotland. These mandalas incorporate intricate knotwork and symbols, representing the cyclical nature of life and the interplay between the physical and spiritual realms.
- In the Western esoteric tradition, mandalas have been employed in many forms of divination and as a technique of focusing the mind during meditation. They can be produced using natural materials such as stones or leaves or painted on canvas.

It is possible to make them by using geometric patterns, or you may incorporate some symbolic components like numerals, animals, deities, or astrological signs.

Regardless of the exact cultural context in which they are created, mandalas are typically understood to be symbolic representations of the universe as well as instruments for the development of the spirituality of oneself.

It is claimed that they can facilitate personal development and create inner peace; hence, they are frequently employed as the focal point in meditation and visualization practices. In general, the shape of a mandala is mainly governed not just by the reason for which it is being produced, but also by the religious or cultural tradition in which it is being employed.

A Mandala can be anything we want it to be, a beautiful art piece, a tool to heal and meditate, a magical connection to the Divine, or all the above at the same time. In my experience working and creating unique mandalas for my clients, which are based on their internal awareness, and soul evolution at the time of the design, the more I have realized, they connect us to a Higher level of Consciousness.

The mandalas speak to us in messages that some days can be heard in our mind, other times; it is a subtle message that is more felt in our hearts or soul. In the case of my design, the more one looks at it, the more one will discover things they had not noticed before.

No matter what aspect we choose, looking at mandalas does not leave us indifferent, as they are the language of our soul. They bring internal changes and lead us to ultimate inner peace and serenity over time.

Throughout history, mandalas have been recognized for their profound healing properties. When we engage with mandalas, whether by creating or meditating upon them, we tap into their transformative energy and open ourselves up to healing on a deep soul level. Mandalas can help us release emotional blockages, find inner peace, and gain clarity and insight.

In our modern world, where stress, anxiety, and disconnection are prevalent, sacred mandalas offer a powerful antidote. By immersing ourselves in the history and origins of mandalas, we can rediscover their ancient wisdom and harness their healing vibrations to awaken our souls and embark on a transformative journey of self-discovery and healing.

Symbolism and Significance of Mandalas in Healing and Transformation

Symbolism and Significance of Mandalas in Healing and Transformation

The power of symbolism and the significance of mandalas in the realm of healing and transformation is profound. In the quest for self-discovery and inner growth, individuals seeking healing and yearning to follow their soul's vibration often find solace and guidance in the sacred art of mandalas.

A sacred mandala is not just a beautiful geometric design; it is a portal to the depths of our subconscious and a vessel through which we can connect with our higher self. These intricate patterns, often circular in shape, represent the wholeness and interconnectedness of all things. Each line, curve, and color hold a specific meaning, serving as a bridge between the conscious and unconscious mind.

The symbolism within mandalas is deeply rooted in ancient wisdom and spiritual traditions. The circle, with its infinite nature, represents the eternal cycle of life, death, and rebirth. It is a symbol of unity and completeness, reminding us that we are part of a larger cosmic tapestry. The intricate patterns within the mandala reflect the complexities of our own lives, reminding us that even during chaos, there is order and harmony to be found.

Engaging with mandalas can be a transformative journey for the soul. As we immerse ourselves in their intricate designs, we enter a meditative state that allows us to access deeper levels of consciousness. By focusing our attention on the mandala's center and following its intricate patterns, we create a sense of stillness and focus within ourselves. This meditative practice helps us quiet the mind, release stress, and tap into our inner wisdom.

The healing power of mandalas is multifaceted. They can aid in emotional healing, helping individuals process and release trauma, grief, and emotional blockages. By engaging with the mandala's symbols and colors, we can bring balance back into our lives and restore our energetic flow.

Furthermore, mandalas can also serve as a tool for spiritual healing. They can awaken dormant aspects of our soul, allowing us to connect with our higher self and access spiritual insights. Through the contemplation of mandalas, we can embark on a sacred journey of self-discovery, unlocking our true potential and aligning with our soul's purpose.

Depending on the cultural or spiritual tradition to which the mandala is being adapted, as well as the ideas or messages the artist seeks to express, the mandala can be embellished with a wide variety of symbols.

Some potential symbols for a mandala are as follows:

Circles, triangles, squares, and hexagons are all examples of geometric shapes that are frequently employed in mandalas to create patterns and give the artwork deeper significance.

Animals: Birds, dragons, and serpents are just some examples of animals that can be incorporated into a mandala to represent the divine or stand in for a particular quality.

Symbols of development, renewal, and a re-connection with nature are often featured in mandalas by using elements of nature such as flowers, trees, and mountains.

Symbols of certain deities or divine figures may be included in mandalas; however, this will vary from one cultural or spiritual tradition to another.

These emblems might call upon the god's presence or identify with his or her unique characteristics.

Mandalas may include religious texts such as mantras or prayers from certain cultures to further enhance their significance.

In general, a mandala's symbols will be determined by the artist's intended themes and meanings.

Each person's mandala will be unique because it will have symbols that speak to their own personal interests and spiritual values from among the vast array of possibilities.

Let s start by quoting some famous authors to dwell deeper into the symbolism and spiritualism of Mandalas and why it is very important for each one of us to connect with them by re-centering ourselves and remembering our Divine Essence even though we are living in a human vessel.

"The mandala emphasizes the process of spiritual growth, of the mind's evolution, echoing the evolution of the universe."
Todd Siler, Breaking the Mind Barrier

This phrase wonderfully summarizes the mandala and its significance in our quest for enlightenment. Mandalas are not simply pretty pictures; they are also potent symbols that stand for the development of the individual's spirit and intellect. Working with mandalas allows us to access our innate knowledge and develop a more holistic view of our role in the cosmos.

The mandala's circular form represents the linked nature of all things and conveys a sense of totality and completion. The mandala's intricate patterns and symbols act as a guide on the path to enlightenment, leading us to a place of calmer, more introspective contemplation.

By making and meditating on mandalas, we can open ourselves to a higher state of awareness and strengthen our connection to the divine.

If you go into your garden, you may feel yourself present in the divine embrace right there in the presence of a golden sunflower with a mandala for its center – the Immanence of the Transcendent in the flower." Marion Woodman and Elinor Dickson, Dancing in the Flames, the Dark Goddess in the Transformation of Consciousness

The above quote highlights the possibility of having a holy experience during our everyday routine and enjoying the present moment.

A sunflower with a mandala at its center symbolizes the ability to recognize the transcendent in the material world. These ideas are symbolized by mandalas, which can be circular images expressing wholeness and the divinity within everyone. In their book "Dancing in the Flames," authors Woodman and Dickson suggest that being totally present and aware of one's surroundings might lead to a sense of the divine.

Due to its abundance of life and beauty, a garden can make us feel as though we are being held by the supernatural. The mandala in the flower's core represents the transcendent as immanent or present, in our lives and in the universe at large. This idea inspires us to look for the sacred in everyday life and to find beauty in everything. In doing so, it encourages us to connect with people and live in the now.

Swiss psychiatrist and pioneer of analytical psychology, Carl Jung was captivated by mandalas and considered them significant symbolism in the path of individuation, or the process of coming into one's own. Jung thought mandalas embodied the principles of the unconscious mind's ability to self-regulate, and he thought that making one could be a technique to access the unconscious and bring unconscious content to the surface.

He theorized that working with mandalas could be a means to integrate these unconscious parts and attain a greater sense of unity and wholeness and that the process of constructing a mandala could expose the individual's unconscious conflicts and archetypes.

Jung also believed that mandalas might help people find inner peace and harmony by serving as a conduit between their conscious and unconscious selves.

He frequently encouraged his patients to make mandalas as a means of gaining insight into their unconscious processes and exploring their inner worlds because he believed that the act of making a mandala may be therapeutic and transforming…

Overall, Jung's work with mandalas was an important part of his psychology, and he saw them as a valuable tool for self-exploration and personal growth.

*"**The mandala is an archetypal image whose occurrence is attested throughout the ages. It signifies the wholeness of the Self. This circular image represents the wholeness of the psychic ground or, to put it in mythic terms, the divinity incarnates in man.**"*

Carl Jung's Memories, Dreams, and Reflections
Pages 334-335

Carl Jung's words emphasize the evergreen and transcendent value of mandalas. It is Jung's contention that the mandala is an archetypal image that recurs across time and cultures. This design, which incorporates both the unconscious and the conscious, is circular to symbolize the completeness of the Self. In a simpler way, the mandala represents the full and balanced union of one's mind, body, and soul.

It was Jung's contention that the mandala personifies the "psychic ground," or the core of an individual's identity. As Jung puts it, "the divinity incarnates in man," therefore this communion with the innermost parts of one's being is revered as holy and heavenly.

This is how the mandala can remind us of our inherent divinity and our oneness with all of creation. In summary, this quote shows how significant mandalas are as metaphors for the development of one's own inner wisdom and spirituality.

Individuals can access their own inner wisdom and experience a deeper sense of harmony and wholeness by meditating on and connecting with the mandala's archetypal images. Working with mandalas can be a technique to attain greater balance and harmony inside the mind, which, according to Jung, is centered on the mandala.

"Immortality is a clock that never runs down, a mandala that revolves eternally like the heavens." Carl Jung, Collected Works

This phrase alludes to the timelessness and eternal nature of mandalas.

The mandala, with its geometric design that radiates outward from a center point, depicts the infinite and unending cycle of creation and destruction, birth, and death, and light and dark. Accessing this timeless knowledge through mandalas gives us a feeling of immortality and belonging to something greater than ourselves.

In this sense, the mandala serves as a reminder of our place in the big scheme of things and enables us to find meaning and purpose in our life.

As we go deeper into the world of mandalas, and their importance in the Earth Realm, it is worth exploring in more detail some of the unique and elaborate patterns found in ancient temples.

Chapter 2

Exploring the Soul's Vibration

Connecting with the Inner Self

Connecting with the Inner Self

Mandalas can be a potent tool for deepening one's relationship with the natural world and for discovering its wondrous depths and intricate patterns. It has been said that making or looking at a mandala that features scenes from nature can help one feel more in one with nature and the divine.

However, deep within each of us lies a sacred space, a place of pure potential and inner wisdom. It is within this space that we can connect with our inner self, and our soul›s vibration, and embark on a profound healing journey.

Connecting with the Inner Self is a gateway to rediscovering the power and magic that resides within you. It explores the transformative journey of sacred mandalas and how they can serve as a catalyst for healing and connecting with your soul's vibration. By engaging with these mandalas, you can enter a state of deep relaxation and open yourself up to the wisdom and guidance of your inner self. Each of the different types of mandalas explained below has its own vibration and will resonate with each one of you on an individual level.

Different types of Mandalas

The Mandala of the Dendera Temple in Egypt.

During my trip to Egypt in 2020, I was able to visit several historic temples, but what I experienced at the Dendera complex will stay with me forever.

This temple is proof of the extraordinary skills of the ancient master builders, which seems to have been lost in time as today we are not able to reproduce their knowledge and technics, but it also contains an incredible collection of symbolism and mandalas in a single location.

The mandalas of the Dendera style are unlike any other and cannot be replicated. Instead of being straightforward geometric patterns, they are intricate multi-tiered carvings that highlight astrological themes and signs.

Perhaps the most well-known of these mandalas is the Dendera Zodiac. The zodiac signs and the night sky are depicted in a circular format.

The Dendera Zodiac is of outstanding significance not only because of its artistic appeal but also because of the incredible attention to detail that went into creating it. It is believed that this mandala has a history that spans more than 2,000 years; if this is indeed the case, and then it would be one of the earliest depictions of the zodiac ever discovered. The fact that it has been maintained for such a long time and is still in such good condition is evidence of both the artisanship and reverence with which it was fashioned when it was first created.

When I looked at the Dendera Zodiac, I was amazed by the incredible precision and position of the astrological symbols.

Could the ancient Egyptians predict the future? Were they aware of the precise positions of the stars, planets, and other celestial bodies in the sky? Were they tapping into something more fundamental, which was not restricted by the constraints of the limits of time or space? I will let you decide for yourself.

The Dendera Zodiac is a metaphor for the perpetual and recurring patterns that are visible in both life and the cosmos. This metaphor can be regarded as a representation of the Dendera Zodiac.

As I stood in this temple, surrounded by these beautiful mandalas, I was reminded that we are all connected to something more solid, something that transcends each of our individual lives and connects us to the cosmos.

Mandala from India

Since their beginning in India, mandalas have been used to provide divine guidance, help emotional healing, and achieve inner change. From the bustling streets of Mumbai to the quiet mountain villages of the Himalayas, mandalas can be found in a variety of forms and styles throughout India.

It is a visual representation of higher thoughts with deeper meaning, and when analyzed closely, one can see, feel, and sometimes even hear hidden messages from the different beings that helped create the mandala.

Additionally, it shows the divine powers at work in the universe, it represents the wonders found on earth, as well as in our curious mind, and is considered to bring about spiritual enlightenment via the practice of meditation.

Mandalas, with their elaborate geometric designs, have been an integral part of Indian culture for thousands of years. In India, mandalas are seen as more than just pretty patterns; they are compelling tools for each individual spiritual evolution and transformation. They offer a window into the infinite understanding of the universe, allowing us to connect with the divine and tap into our innermost desires and beliefs.

Therefore, the mandalas of India should not be ignored by anyone who is either spiritually curious or who enjoys the beauty of ancient art forms.

I encourage you to experience the immense power and beauty of the mandala by visiting the place where it all began, in Tibet whether virtually or in person...

The mandalas of India will move your heart and inspire your soul whether you encounter them in a temple, a meditation center, or on the street.

Tree of Life Mandala

Ah, the tree of life in mandalas - what a beautiful and symbolic representation of growth, renewal, and the interconnections of all things. Just like the branches of a tree reach upward to the sky and the roots delve deep into the earth, the tree of life in mandalas symbolizes our connection to both the celestial realm and the physical world.

Each branch and root of the tree of life in a mandala represents a different aspect of our being and our journey through life. The branches might symbolize our aspirations, our hopes, and our dreams. The roots might symbolize our grounding, our connection to the earth and to our ancestors, and our sense of belonging to something greater than ourselves.

Moreover, just like a tree, we too are always growing and changing. We shed our old leaves and grow new ones, just as we shed our old beliefs and embrace new perspectives. The tree of life in a mandala reminds us that growth is a constant process and that there is always something new to discover and explore.

In meditation and contemplation, the tree of life in a mandala can serve as a powerful tool for personal transformation and spiritual growth. By focusing on the intricate branches and roots, we can connect to our deepest desires, fears, and aspirations. We can release what no longer serves us and embrace new possibilities.

So next time you come across a mandala featuring the tree of life, take a moment to pause and reflect and choose to grow and evolve.

The Flower of Life Mandala

The Flower of Life mandala, widely regarded as one of the most mesmerizing and mysterious of all mandalas, has been baffling people's minds for centuries.

It is like discovering a secret garden full of beautiful patterns and symbols that fill you with wonder and a sense of the supernatural, like a garden of holy geometry.

Just looking at the Flower of Life can hypnotize you with its fascinating beauty. Closer scrutiny of this mandala, however, exposes a wealth of extra intricacy.

It is said to hold timeless insight into the meaning of life, the cosmos, and the interdependence of all things.

The flower's individual petals each stand for a distinct stage in the creative process, and the overlapping circles stand for the cohesion and balance that may be found among all things.

It is believed that the Flower of Life is also a pattern of the universe, with each petal representing a different facet of creation. These aspects include the planets, the elements, and the cosmos, among other things.

This mandala is meant to serve as a constant reminder that everything in the cosmos is interconnected and that every one of us is an integral part of something much larger.

By meditating on the Flower of Life, we can connect with the cosmic consciousness and achieve a greater awareness of the vastness of the cosmos as well as our position within it.

The practice of meditating on the Flower of Life can help us connect with our higher selves and the divine, as well as bring a sense of calm and tranquility into our lives.

It is like a key that lets us in on the mysteries of the cosmos and can put us on the path to achieving enlightenment on a spiritual level as well as personal growth.

Therefore, the next time you come across the Flower of Life, pause for a moment and let its power work its wonders on you.

Allow its splendor and enlightenment to serve as a gentle reminder of the sanctity of life and the boundless opportunities that are available across the cosmos.

Hawaiian Mandala

la'a kea, the Hawaiian word for sacred light, and A'o kahua 'Uhane is used to illustrate spiritual learning. Nature, including plants, animals, elements, and symbols of the gods and ancestors, are common components of Hawaiian mandalas.

Hawaiian mandalas are often made from organic materials like shells, feathers, and stones, and serve as meditation focal points or conduits for spiritual communion with the natural world.

Mandalas have an important role in the spiritual practices of the Hawaiian people, who employ them in rites and ceremonies to pay homage to the ancestors and the divine.

Traditional media such as paint or pencil can also be utilized to construct Hawaiian mandalas, which can then be used for artistic expression or to delve further into spiritual concepts and ideas.

The spiritual traditions of the Hawaiian people and their ties to the natural world provide the basis for a rich and complex symbol system that is expressed in mandalas.

Hoponopono mandala

In Hawaii, there is a tradition called ho'oponopono that aims to bring people together through the power of forgiveness and restitution practiced with the aid of a mandala.

The mandala serves as a metaphor for the release of negative emotions and the cultivation of positive ones in this environment.

If you want to make a Hoponopono mandala, you may start by picking out some colors and symbols that represent the feelings of compassion and restoration that you hope to evoke.

Flowers and trees, both symbols of growth and rebirth, could be used in the mandala. Symbols of the divine, such as the sun or a star, could also be included, as they are often looked to for direction and inspiration.

A mantra or prayer, such as "I am sorry, please forgive me, thank you, I love you," may be said by the practitioner as the mandala is being made to help focus their thoughts and connect with the aim of forgiveness and healing.

The act of making a mandala can be a form of meditation and therapy, as well as a means of increasing one's supply of happy emotions.

Forgiveness, healing, and personal development are at the heart of the Hoponopono mandala, which has its origins in Hawaiian spirituality.

Making a Hoponopono mandala can help you focus on the good and release the bad, leading to more happiness and calm.

Mandala in nature

Nature is revered as a divine expression and a source of inspiration in a wide range of religious and philosophical traditions.

Many people turn to mandalas as a means of connecting with the natural world and of conveying its beauty and complexity to others.

Among the many possible applications of mandalas to depicting the natural world are the following:

Nature is often the subject of mandalas, both in terms of the materials used to build them (such as feathers and stones) and the subjects depicted (including flowers, trees, and animals).

Mandalas can be made with geometric patterns that are based on or reminiscent of natural patterns present in the world around us, such as the patterns found in seashells, or the patterns formed by ripples in water.

Making a mandala can be a means to illustrate the interdependence of all things in nature, and mandalas can incorporate a broad variety of natural components and patterns.

Through step-by-step instructions and exercises, you will learn how to tap into your intuition and connect with your inner self on a profound level.

By incorporating self-care practices into your daily routine, you can create a harmonious balance within yourself and cultivate a deep connection with your soul›s vibration.

Whether you are seeking healing from past traumas, searching for direction in your life, or simply looking to deepen your connection with your inner self, connecting with the Inner Self is a guidebook that will support and empower you on your healing journey. Through the transformative power of sacred mandalas and the exploration of self-care practices, you will awaken your soul's vibration and embark on a profound journey of healing and transformation.

Discovering the Soul's Purpose and Passion

Discovering the Soul's Purpose and Passion

There comes a time in each of our lives when we feel called to look inward and ask more profound questions. "What is my purpose?" "Why am I here?" In our fast-paced modern world, these questions often go unanswered as we hurry through our days without pause. Yet our souls yearn for us to slow down, quiet the mind, and listen to the whispers of our inner truth.

The sacred mandalas found within this book offer a doorway to self-discovery. As we reflect on their patterns and vibrant hues, we initiate a journey to the core of our being. These mandalas resonate and align with our energy centers, known as chakras in ancient traditions. When we focus on a mandala, we stimulate our chakras and open pathways to our soul's wisdom.

1. Root Chakra (Muladhara): The "Root Rockstar." Located at the base of your spine, this chakra keeps you grounded like a sturdy tree. It is all about stability, security, and feeling at home in your body. Imagine roots spreading deep into the earth, giving you a solid foundation to rock your world.

2. Sacral Chakra (Swadhisthana): The "Creative Firecracker." Nestled in your lower abdomen, this chakra ignites your passion and fuels your creativity. It is a burst of vibrant orange energy that dances within you, encouraging self-expression and pleasure. Unleash your inner firecracker and let your creative juices flow!
3. Solar Plexus Chakra (Manipura): The "Confidence Dynamo." Located in your upper abdomen, this chakra radiates bright yellow energy, boosting your self-esteem and personal power. It is like your internal sunshine, empowering you to shine your unique light in the world. Feel the fire of your confidence and let it light up your path.
4. Heart Chakra (Anahata): The "Love Luminary." Found at the center of your chest, this chakra is all about love, compassion, and connection. It beams a soothing green light that embraces you and others, reminding you of the beautiful interplay of hearts. Let love be your guiding star and watch it ripple through your life.
5. Throat Chakra (Vishuddha): The "Communication Maestro." Nestled in your throat, this chakra is like a sparkling blue microphone, empowering your voice and authentic expression. It encourages clear communication, heartfelt conversations, and the power to speak your truth. Grab the mic and let your voice soar!
6. Third Eye Chakra (Ajna): The "Intuition Magician." Situated between your eyebrows, this chakra opens the door to your inner wisdom and intuition. It is like a majestic indigo portal that connects you to higher realms and reveals hidden truths. Trust your inner magician and embrace the magic of your intuitive knowing.
7. Crown Chakra (Sahasrara): The "Divine Dreamer." Sitting at the top of your head, this chakra is your gateway to the cosmic realm. It is like a majestic violet crown, connecting you to divine wisdom and the vastness of the universe. Tap into the infinite possibilities and embrace the divine dreamer within you.

Each chakra is a vibrant aspect of your being, inviting you to explore and harmonize your energy. So, let the colors, energies, and playful descriptions of these chakras inspire you to embark on a journey of self-discovery and holistic well-being. Embrace your inner rockstar, firecracker, luminary, maestro, magician, and dreamer. Let your chakra dance shine!

Imagine your consciousness as a tuning fork, absorbing the mandala's vibration. Feel as if your entire being comes into harmonic resonance with each mandala. Breathe deeply and allow your mind to be still. Pay attention to the sensations, thoughts, and insights that arise. You may uncover hidden passions, talents, and desires that have lain dormant within you.

Your soul's purpose is waiting patiently to be revealed. It is not something to chase after or acquire. Rather, it is a seed encoded in your very essence. This book outlines a path to water that seeds through meditation, self-awareness practices, and conscious living.

When we have the courage to look within and honor our soul's longing, our lives become infused with joy and meaning. Our soul's purpose is fulfilled when we have the faith to follow its quiet guidance, moment by moment. We awaken to discover that we already possess everything required for the journey ahead.

Aligning with the Soul's Vibration for Healing and Transformation

Aligning with the Soul's Vibration for Healing and Transformation

In the midst of our chaotic and fast-paced lives, it is easy to lose touch with our true selves, like losing the TV remote in the couch cushions.

Awakening the Soul's Vibration: Sacred Mandalas for Healing and Transformation

We often find ourselves disconnected from our inner voice, yearning for healing and transformation like a phone desperately needing a reboot. If you are someone in need of healing, looking to tune into your soul's frequency, then this is tailored just for you.

Everything in our universe vibrates at its own unique frequency, resonating in harmony with the symphony of creation. Our souls too have their own distinct energetic vibration, often referred to as the soul's tune. When we can align with and attune to the frequency of our soul, we gain access to our inner wisdom, creativity, and purpose.

Sacred mandalas hold the remarkable power to put us in vibrational resonance with our highest soul frequency. These ancient symbols contain precise geometric patterns that mirror the harmonics of nature, creation, and the cosmos.

As we gently focus our gaze on a mandala, its intricacies and radiant color codes begin to still our busy minds. Our breath deepens and our bodies relax. In this calm, open state, our energetic field, or aura becomes receptive to the mandala's vibration. Its frequency gently entrains our own, allowing our soul's tune to come through, clear and strong.

Imagine your consciousness as a radio receiver, constantly tuned to the cacophony of the outer world. The incessant mental chatter and distraction keep us perpetually out of tune with our soul frequency. A sacred mandala functions like a master dial, perfectly calibrating our inner radio to pick up the divine signal of our soul.

As we set our intention, the mandala tunes the dials with just the right geometric precision to home in on our unique frequency. The colorful designs begin to shimmer and pulse, sending a resonance code into our being. Suddenly, we detect our soul's vibration arising within like a favorite childhood song. Our entire body-mind relaxes into this harmony and begins radiating the soul's tune.

Working with sacred mandalas awakens our consciousness to the divine music that is always singing within us and throughout nature. Their geometric codes and vibrant colors align us with the sacred foundations of life, opening portals to self-realization, creativity, and purpose. Through this attunement to our soul's vibration, we remember how to receive its limitless guidance, intuitive knowledge, and healing light.

The journey toward healing and transformation begins by understanding the profound power of sacred mandalas, like magical carpets that can fly us to our soul's destination. These intricate and mesmerizing patterns have been used for centuries as a tool for self-discovery and spiritual growth, like ancient maps guiding us inward. They serve as a gateway to the depths of our souls, offering insights and revelations that can guide us toward wholeness, like diving down into an underwater treasure chest.

By immersing yourself in the world of sacred mandalas, you embark on a healing journey for your soul, like boarding a plane to your soul's home country. These divine symbols act as a mirror, reflecting your innermost desires, fears, and aspirations, like a crystal ball revealing your soul's truths. They hold the key to unlocking your true potential and aligning with your soul's vibration, like a secret password that lets you access your soul's gifts.

The art of using sacred mandalas for healing and transformation is like learning to wield a magic paintbrush that transforms your inner world. We explore various techniques and practices that will help you tap into the vibrational energy of your soul, like tuning your soul's radio dial to just the right frequency. Through guided meditations and visualizations, you will learn to quiet the noise of the external world and listen to the gentle whispers of your inner being, like turning down the world's volume knob so you can hear your soul's song.

Moreover, the importance of self-care and self-compassion in the healing process is like giving yourself a soothing hug when you need it most. Nurturing your mind, body, and spirit is essential for aligning with your soul's vibration, like keeping your soul's instrument in tune. I offer practical tips and exercises that will assist you in creating a sacred space for yourself, where you can recharge and reconnect with your deepest self.

Let the sacred mandalas be your compass as you embark on this remarkable journey toward healing and transformation, like a cosmic GPS guiding you home to your soul.

Chapter 3

Healing Through Mandalas

Mandalas as a Tool for Emotional Healing

We live in an age of fragmentation that has severed our connection to wholeness. In our fixation on rapid progress, we have numbed ourselves to the gentle calling of our souls. However, a lifeline to reunion with our essential nature is woven into the living fabric of the Universe. To retrieve our souls' vast wisdom, we need only pause, quiet our minds, and tune into their frequencies once more.

We often cruise through life in the fast lane, hustling to cross things off our to-do lists, unaware that we are drowning out the gentle hum of our souls. However, within each of us dwells an inner compass guiding us toward growth and wholeness - our soul's unique vibration. To hear its whisper and experience deep healing, we need only pause and tune into its frequency.

The sacred mandala offers a gateway to this soulful attunement. At first glance, these circular designs bursting with color and geometry may seem merely decorative. But they are portals to self-discovery crafted by ancient sages to awaken our highest potential.

For centuries across cultures, mandalas have guided seekers inward to harvest their soul's wisdom. These cosmic maps hold an energetic resonance that stills the chatter of the mind. As we trace their patterns, our breath deepens, and we enter a meditative space ideal for releasing that, which no longer serves us.

Those nursing tender wounds or weathered by life's storms can find shelter in the mandala's eye. It is centering shape and vibrant hues reorient us to our wholeness. Fear and pain naturally soften as we remember our unbreakable life force.

The mandala's healing alchemy works gently yet powerfully. With a brush or pencil, we can color its forms, watching our emotions mirror back to us on the page. Alternatively, softly gazing at its circular geometry, we may feel energy meridians open, and chakras harmonize.

As we learn to listen to the mandala's vibration, we also tune into the song of the Universe singing within us all. Healing is no longer a solo act but a sacred dance with something greater than we are.

Awakening the Soul's Vibration is a wise and nurturing guide to this soulful journey. It unveils the transformative power of mandalas through practical exercises, meditations, and journaling.

When we dare to hear and be the music of our souls, our lives become art that moves, inspires, and heals. The mandala is an ancient technology for soulful attunement, used by mystics across millennia to awaken human potential. At first glimpse, these circular designs seem merely decorative, and pleasing to the eye. But they are sacred portals designed to transport us to an awakened state of unity consciousness.

Geometry is the language the Universe uses to orchestrate the cosmos, dictating the dance between planets, stars, and galaxies. The mandala's perfect symmetry reflects the harmonic ratios that undergird all of creation. To gaze upon one is to glimpse the hidden perfection dwelling in everything, waiting to be revealed.

The mandala's geometric frequencies generate a resonance field that stills the incessant chatter of our monkey minds. As we contemplate its patterns, our breathing returns to its natural rhythm, and alpha brain waves ripple through our nervous system. We enter a meditative space where we are receptive to release that which binds us.

For those weighed down by anxiety, anger, or grief, the mandala is a refuge. Its concentric forms beckon us to our center point of stillness, providing 360 degrees of perspective. Its vivid hues reflect back the light of our inner joy, helping us remember we each hold an infinite wellspring of life.

Creating mandalas is a powerful act of soulful alchemy. With mindful brushstrokes, we anchor our emotions into the design, transforming them through sacred geometry. What emerges often reveals guidance from our intuitive wisdom.

In the mandala's presence, our individual consciousness synchronizes with the Universal flow. No longer isolated, we become conduits of a vast living intelligence seeking expression through us all. Our souls awaken us to behold the beauty that unfolds when we create in harmony with Life's organizing principles.

Mandalas for Physical Healing and Well-being

Mandalas for Physical Healing and Well-being

In the quest for holistic healing and well-being, exploring the world of sacred mandalas can be a transformative and enlightening journey. Mandalas, with their intricate and symmetrical designs, have been used for centuries as powerful tools for spiritual growth, meditation, and self-discovery. But did you know that mandalas could also be instrumental in physical healing?

The mandala's healing potential unfolds in layers, as we devote ourselves to diving deeper into its mysteries. The longer we immerse in its frequencies, the more its energies work their alchemy, rewriting outmoded patterns in our cells. Old belief systems that limited us fade away as we awaken to our unlimited potential.

Each mandala has unique architecture that engages specific energetics. Some feature geometric forms that mirror the repeating patterns throughout nature. Contemplating these designs reminds us of the sacrality infusion into all things and our unity with the web of life.

Other mandalas incorporate ancient symbols with their particular vibrational signatures. The flower of life shape, for example, signifies divine perfection at the heart of every soul. Its petals open us to receive higher guidance from our eternal nature.

We all have mandalas whose designs most closely resonate with our energy. Make time for stillness and reflection, allowing your intuition to guide you to the mandalas you are called to work with now. Notice how you feel as you hold your awareness of each one. The mandalas that enliven you and instill a sense of expansion are those your soul recognizes.

Crafting and contemplating mandalas is a practice in presence that ripens our consciousness. Their sacred forms reattune us to stillness, realign us with Source energy, and unleash our creative potential in service to the world. In their grace, we remember we are both the artists and the art, the healers and those being healed.

For those in need of healing, who are looking to follow their soul's vibration, these sacred mandalas can be a beacon of hope and a source of profound transformation.

Physical healing starts with acknowledging the intricate connection between the body, mind, and soul. Sacred mandalas offer a unique pathway to tap into this connection and harness the body's natural healing capabilities. By meditating on these mandalas, individuals can unlock their inner healing energies, allowing them to flow freely and restore balance to the body.

The patterns and colors found in mandalas for physical healing are carefully chosen to resonate with specific energy centers, known as chakras, within the body. These energy centers are believed to hold the key to our overall health and well-being. Through focused meditation on these mandalas, individuals can align and balance their chakras, promoting physical healing on a deep, cellular level.

Furthermore, mandalas for physical healing are often infused with sacred symbols and geometric patterns that activate the body's natural healing response. These symbols act as energetic catalysts, stimulating the body's innate ability to heal itself. As individuals immerse themselves in the vibrational frequencies of these mandalas, they can experience a profound sense of relaxation, release, and rejuvenation.

Whether you are seeking relief from physical ailments, looking to optimize your health, or simply embarking on a journey of self-discovery, mandalas for physical healing and well-being are a valuable resource. By embracing the power of these sacred symbols, you can tap into your body's innate wisdom and embark on a transformative healing journey that aligns with your soul's vibration.

Mandalas for Spiritual Healing and Connection

Mandalas for Spiritual Healing and Connection

In today's fast-paced world, many people are seeking solace and healing for their weary souls. They yearn for a deeper connection to themselves and the divine, hoping to find a sense of inner peace and harmony. If you are one of these individuals in need of healing and longing to follow your soul's vibration, sacred mandalas offer a transformative journey that can help you achieve just that.

Mandalas have been used for centuries as a powerful tool for spiritual growth, healing, and self-discovery. Derived from the ancient Sanskrit word meaning "circle," mandalas represent the interconnectedness of all creation. They are intricate geometric designs that serve as a visual representation of the universe and the eternal flow of energy.

Embarking on a sacred mandala-healing journey for your soul can be a profound experience. Through the creation or contemplation of mandalas, you can tap into your inner wisdom and connect with the higher realms of consciousness. Mandalas provide a sacred space where you can explore your emotions, release negative energies, and invite healing energies to flow through you.

Let us not be weighed down by spiritual seriousness. The journey to enlightenment does not require somber rigidity, but rather playful flexibility. Our souls yearn to dance and delight in life's divine mysteries. This is the wisdom whispered through the mandala's enchanting symmetries and colors. Its mere image reminds us to approach the sacred with wonder and levity.

Picture the cosmos itself erupting into being from divine playfulness. As God, the Supreme Artist, giggled mischievously, POOF - a supernova burst with splendor! Another chuckle - WHOOSH - a billion galaxies swirled into form! We are the stuff of Divine Laughter rippling throughout the Universe.

Now gaze into the Sri Yantra mandala's joyful geometry. Witness its five interlacing triangles chortling together in cosmic camaraderie. "We're all connected!" they seem to say. "We're all part of the same sacred comedy!" Their uproar sends shockwaves of mirthful energy outward in concentric waves.

At the center, behold the four lotus petals gently quivering with the Buddha's belly laugh that sparked it all. His guffaw still tickles the tendrils of our soul's millennia later, inviting us to join in the joke. Every being, every atom, shares one giant inner smile.

As we meditate with a playful heart's eye on the mandala's harmonics, we enter its abode of laughter. Cellular walls soften. Fear and worry unclench their grip. Even time releases its severity, unwinding the clock's hands.

We have found the holy grails of enlightenment and chuckles to be the same chalice, filled with eternal joy. So, drink deeply, and ascend with a spirit of celebration. The cosmos is awaiting your next wisecrack! Whether you are an artist seeking a creative outlet for self-expression or an individual in need of emotional and spiritual healing, this subchapter will guide you on a sacred journey of self-discovery. By incorporating mandalas into your daily practices, you can awaken your soul's vibration and embark on a transformative path toward healing, connection, and self-realization.

Chapter 4

Creating Sacred Mandalas

Materials and Tools for Mandala Creation

Materials and Tools for Mandala Creation

Creating mandalas can be a powerful and transformative experience on the journey of healing and self-discovery. The process of designing and coloring mandalas allows individuals to tap into their inner creativity, connect with their soul's vibration, and find solace and healing in the sacred geometry of these intricate designs. To embark on this sacred mandala-healing journey, it is essential to gather the right materials and tools that will aid in the process of creation.

One of the primary materials required for mandala creation is sturdy drawing paper, canvas, or a sketchbook. It is crucial to choose high-quality paper that can withstand various mediums such as colored pencils, markers, or even watercolors. A larger paper size, such as 11x14 or larger, provides ample space to express your creativity and allows for intricate detailing.

Next, a set of high-quality colored pencils, watercolors, or markers is essential to bring your mandala to life. The choice of colors is entirely personal and can be guided by your intuition and the emotions you wish to express or heal. Vibrant and soothing colors such as blues, purples, and greens are often chosen for their calming and healing properties. Experimenting with different color combinations can evoke different emotions and energies within your mandala.

For those interested in exploring watercolors, a set of watercolor paints and brushes can be a wonderful addition to your mandala toolkit. The fluidity and transparency of watercolors can add depth and dimension to your designs, allowing for a more ethereal and dreamy appearance.

In addition to coloring tools, a compass, and a ruler are essential tools for creating precise and symmetrical mandalas. These tools help in drawing intricate circles, lines, and geometric patterns, ensuring that your mandala reflects the harmonious balance that is often associated with sacred geometry.

Finally, consider incorporating additional elements such as metallic pens or glitter for added sparkle, or even natural materials like dried flowers, leaves, or crystals to infuse your mandala with earthy and grounding energies. You can even add light language symbols to your masterpiece.

Remember, the materials and tools you choose should resonate with your own unique journey of healing and transformation. Allow your intuition to guide you as you select the materials that best align with your soul's vibration. Embrace the process of creating sacred mandalas and let them become a powerful tool for healing and self-expression on your journey of awakening the soul's vibration.

Step-by-Step Guide to Creating Personalized Mandalas

Let's mention Leonardo Da Vinci very briefly before we go into more detail on the basic design of the mandala.

Leonardo da Vinci

During his lifetime in the 15th and 16th centuries, Italian Renaissance master Leonardo da Vinci accomplished much in the fields of art, invention, and science.

While he did not name them mandalas per se, many of his works feature intricate geometric patterns and shapes.

The iconic Vitruvian Man by Leonardo da Vinci, for instance, portrays the human form within a circle and a square, two basic shapes from sacred geometry.

Due to its use of geometric shapes and patterns to represent divine order and the interconnection of all things, this picture has been compared to a mandala.

The fact that Leonardo da Vinci said "Geometry is the foundation of all painting" implies he thought geometrical knowledge was crucial for making art.

Geometry, in his view, was fundamental to comprehending the form and organization of nature, and so it was essential to the process of making art that portrayed nature.

In addition to its practical applications, Leonardo saw geometry as a window into the laws of nature. An artist's works may be more lifelike and accurate if they were familiar with and used the laws of geometry.

For this reason, geometric principles were the bedrock upon which all forms of artistic expression rested. The spiritual and metaphysical significance of geometric shapes and patterns may explain why Leonardo placed such great emphasis on them in his artwork.

Geometry is employed as a tool for meditation and self-discovery in many spiritual traditions because it is viewed to comprehend the nature of the divine and the cosmos.

Leonardo may have been attempting to forge a relationship with God and investigate more profound spiritual and metaphysical subjects by adding geometric concepts to his artwork.

To sum up, Leonardo da Vinci may be considered an influence on the usage of mandalas in art and spirituality, despite his lack of use of the term "mandala" in his work. He was interested in geometric shapes and patterns and incorporated them into his paintings.

Step-by-Step Guide to Creating Personalized Mandalas

Whether you are seeking healing, looking to connect with your soul›s vibration, or simply intrigued by the beauty and symbolism of mandalas, this step-by-step guide will assist you on your journey.

Step 1: Set an Intention

Begin by setting a clear intention for your mandala creation. Reflect on what you wish to heal or transform in your life. This intention will infuse your mandala with the energy and purpose you desire.

Step 2: Gather Your Materials

Collect all the necessary materials, such as paper, pencils, markers, or paints. Choose colors that resonate with your intention and soul vibration. Consider incorporating sacred symbols or images that hold personal significance for you.

Step 3: Create a Sacred Space

Prepare a serene and sacred space where you can fully immerse yourself in the mandala creation process. Light candles, burn incense or play gentle music to enhance the atmosphere and create a sense of tranquility.

Step 4: Connect with Your Inner Self

Take a few moments to ground yourself and connect with your inner self. Close your eyes, take deep breaths, and allow your thoughts to settle. Tune in to the energy within and feel your soul's vibration resonating throughout your being.

Step 5: Begin Drawing

Start by drawing a central point or circle, representing the core essence of your intention. From this center, let your creativity flow freely. Allow your hand to move intuitively, guiding the shapes and patterns that emerge on the page.

Step 6: Embrace the Process

Remember that the creation of your mandala is a personal and intuitive journey. Do not judge or criticize your artwork; instead, embrace the imperfections and celebrate the unique expression of your soul vibration.

Step 7: Infuse with Love and Healing

As you add colors and symbols to your mandala, infuse each stroke with love and healing energy. Visualize your intention manifesting and allow the vibrational energy to radiate from your creation.

Step 8: Reflect and Meditate

Once your mandala is complete, take a moment to observe and reflect upon it. Sit in meditation and let the energy of your creation wash over you. Notice any emotions or insights that arise during this process.

Step 9: Integration and Transformation

Integrate the healing energy of your mandala into your daily life. Place it in a visible location, use it as a focal point for meditation, or carry a smaller version with you as a reminder of your soul's vibration and the transformation you seek.

Creating personalized mandalas can be a powerful tool for self-exploration, healing, and transformation. By following this step-by-step guide, you will embark on a sacred journey, connecting with your soul's vibration and awakening the healing energy within. Embrace the process, trust your intuition, and let your personalized mandala become a profound catalyst for positive change in your life.

Basic Design: Point and Circle

The basic design can start with a circle and a focal or central point.

Throughout history, the circle has been honored for representing wholeness, continuity, and infinity. The circle is frequently used in mandalas to symbolize infinity or oneness with the divine. It acts as a border around the mandala, giving the whole thing a sense of completion and harmony.

The circle represents completeness, a unified whole, and the feminine principle.

Compassion, intuition, and emotion are all characteristics associated with the feminine, and they are all present in the circle. The circle's association with femininity is reinforced by the fact that it resembles the heart, another symbol of love and connection.

The point, on the other hand, is associated with masculine principles because it stands for the mind, logic, reason, and the ability to think clearly are all traits linked with this word.

One common topic among mandalas is the harmony achieved when the feminine and masculine elements are balanced.

Throughout history, the circle has been honored for representing wholeness, continuity, and infinity. The circle is frequently used in mandalas to symbolize infinity or oneness with the divine. It acts as a border around the mandala, giving the whole thing a sense of completion and harmony.

Meditation using a mandala's point and circle as a focal point is a potent method for expanding one's awareness and strengthening one's spiritual bonds. The divine spark within us, the pure consciousness that transcends the constraints of our physical bodies and the material universe, is commonly represented as the point at the center of the circle.

Exploring a sacred mandala is a powerful means of connecting with and awakening the soul. It is a journey of self-discovery and enlightenment, allowing us to access higher realms of understanding and healing. By visualizing the mandala, we can take a step back from the daily grind and be open to the mystery and beauty of life. Through our meditation, we can transcend the boundaries of our physical reality and reach a more profound state of understanding.

Focusing on the "heart" of the mandala allows us to begin connecting with this innate knowledge and opening up to a higher state of awareness.

Focusing on the point may cause us to feel as though our consciousness is growing past the confines of our bodies and merging with the cosmos at large. The circle, as a metaphor for oneness and infinity, can assist in strengthening this bond. In doing so, it serves as a gentle reminder that our individual lives are intertwined with the bigger cosmic cycles of birth, death, and rebirth. We can deepen our spiritual awareness and feel a sense of oneness with the cosmos by meditating on the mandala's point and circle.

As we open ourselves up to the divine inside and all around us, we may experience inner calm and newfound clarity, as we perceive things from a different perspective.

We can become closer to our authentic selves and the universe's boundless potential with each meditation session.

As humans, we have a built-in desire to look for belonging and connection outside of ourselves, in the hopes that we will discover it in other people or the wider environment.

In hopes of finding the harmony and affection we all want, some of us may look for Mr. or Mrs. Right, or the ideal workplace or community.

But what we tend to overlook is that we have all we need to find harmony and love already within ourselves. There is an infinite supply of love and unity within us, and we may access it by turning inward and focusing on the core of our being.

We can tap into this wellspring of love and oneness by meditating with the aid of mandalas.

The more we zero in on the heart of the matter, the more we see that we are not apart from the world but rather a part of it.

When we begin to understand that the life force that flows through us also flows through all beings, we begin to feel a profound sense of unity and interdependence with all of life.

Although it is human nature to look for love and harmony from without, it is essential to keep in mind that these qualities originate within each of us.

By looking inward, to the center, and the point of focus, we can access the boundless reservoir of love and unity within us and feel a profound bond with the cosmos.

Imagine yourself standing at the edge of a vast ocean, staring out at the horizon. It is easy to feel small and insignificant in the face of such a massive and seemingly endless expanse. But what if you could tap into a deeper consciousness that connects you to the very essence of that ocean?

Focusing on the point of the mandala is like diving into the depths of that ocean. At first, it might seem overwhelming or even scary to let go of the surface and sink deeper. However, as you allow yourself to go deeper, you might start to let go of things that no longer serve you, like rocks you have been carrying in your pockets for far too long.

As we color or create, we are encouraged to focus on the center of the mandala. But have you ever found yourself struggling to do so? That is a sign that maybe you are feeling a little out of balance with yourself and the universe. Nevertheless, don't worry, practicing with mandalas can help you get back in sync. As you release those burdens, you create space for something new to come into your life. It might be a new opportunity, a new relationship, or simply a renewed sense of purpose and joy.

By opening ourselves up to the vulnerability that comes with creating, we allow ourselves to release any negative energies that might be weighing us down. And in doing so, we make room for new and exciting things to come into our lives.

The point of the mandala is not just a physical point, but also a gateway to a higher consciousness that can help you tap into the infinite possibilities of the universe. It can be the beginning of a journey or the culmination of a long and winding path. It all depends on how you approach it, and how willing you are to let go of what no longer serves you.

So, take a deep breath, dive in, and see what new wonders you might discover in the depths.

Square and Triangle

There are many other simple geometric shapes found in mandalas, each with its own spiritual meaning.

When it comes to mandalas, the different shapes and patterns used are like ingredients in a recipe - each one adding its own unique flavor to the mix.

Let's square up and talk about the power of the square in mandalas! The square is a rock-solid shape that brings us stability, security, and grounding in the physical world. Think of it like a reliable friend who is always there for you when you need a sturdy foundation.

But the square is more than just a practical shape. It also represents balance and order, two things that are essential for spiritual growth. Picture a balanced scale, perfectly level and free from any tipping point. The square can be the symbol of that perfect balance that we strive to achieve in our spiritual practice.

And in the world of mandalas, the square has even more meaning. It can be used to represent the four directions, the four elements, or even the four seasons. Each corner of the square can represent a different direction or element, creating a framework for the design and guiding us on our spiritual journey.

So, let's embrace the square and all its stability and balance. It can be a powerful tool in our spiritual practice, providing us with the foundation we need to reach new heights of awareness and consciousness.

On the other hand, Triangles are the cool kids of geometry - they may be the underdogs of basic shapes, but they pack a punch when it comes to spiritual symbolism. The triangle is like the Swiss Army Knife of shapes - it can represent growth, ascension, and the connection between the physical and spiritual realms all at once!

In spiritual traditions, the triangle is like the Holy Trinity, representing the three aspects of the divine. In Hinduism, the triangle is often used to represent Shiva and the three qualities of nature it is as the triangle is the MVP of the shape game.

In mandalas, triangles can be used to create a sense of flow and movement. They can represent the balance between the physical and spiritual worlds. Triangles can also represent the three phases of existence: birth, life, and death, or the three pillars of existence. The upward-facing triangle can symbolize the ascent toward spiritual enlightenment, while the downward-facing triangle can represent the descent into the material world. It is as if the triangle is a ladder to spiritual growth - upwards and onwards!

When triangles join forces with other shapes, like circles or squares, they can create even deeper meanings. A circle with a triangle inside can represent the union of the physical and spiritual worlds. It is as if the triangle is the key to unlocking a cosmic connection. Meanwhile, a square with triangles in each corner can represent the four directions and the elements associated with them.

Hexagon and Octagon

Have you ever stopped to think about the shapes on a mandala and what they might mean? It is not just a bunch of circles and squiggles, my friend. Each shape has its own special significance, and they are not just for nerdy math types to geek out over.

Ah, the mighty hexagon! With its six sides and angles, it is like a six-pack of shapes, except instead of beer, it is full of balance and harmony! The hexagon is the superstar of the heart chakra, which is all about love, compassion, and understanding. It is no wonder that the hexagon is such a powerful tool for meditation, as focusing on its perfect symmetry and balance can help bring balance to your thoughts and emotions.

In the world of mandalas, hexagons can be used to create a sense of interconnections, as each side of the hexagon connects to the others in a harmonious dance. Moreover, let us not forget about the hexagon's gender-bending powers! It represents the union of male and female energies, which is like having both Batman and Wonder Woman on the same team. It is the perfect combination of masculine and feminine energy. Who wouldn't want that kind of balance and harmony in their life?

Let's get ready to octagon! This funky shape brings heat when it comes to regeneration and renewal. With its eight sides and angles, it represents the perfect balance between heaven and earth.

The octagon is like the magical middle ground where the spiritual realm meets the physical world, bringing you the best of both worlds. It's like having your cake and eating it too!

In mandalas, the octagon can create a strong sense of stability and grounding. When combined with other shapes like circles, squares, or triangles, it can help bring a sense of growth and expansion to the design.

Think of the octagon as a trusty sidekick, supporting and balancing everything around it. With its powerful presence, it can help you focus your energy and intentions toward regeneration and renewal.

So, the next time you see an octagon, give it a high five (or an octo-five, if you will) for being such a cool and balanced shape!

So the next time you're creating or coloring a mandala, take a moment to appreciate the shapes and what they represent. Who knows, it might just inspire you to find balance and harmony in your own life,

Simple Lines

Do not underestimate the power of a simple line in mandalas! This little guy can pack a punch in the spiritual realm, as it represents the flow of energy and movement. Think about it - a line can be straight, curved, wavy, thick, thin, and so much more. Each variation can convey a different energy or emotion, such as calmness, excitement, or chaos.

In addition to its representation of movement and energy, the line can also symbolize the journey of life itself. Life is rarely a straight path, and we often encounter twists and turns along the way. By incorporating lines into mandalas, we can visually represent the ups and downs of our journey and remind ourselves to keep moving forward.

So next time you are coloring or drawing a mandala, pay attention to the lines you create. Are they straight and narrow or wild and free? Each line can tell a story, and by being mindful of them, we can better understand our own journey through life.

Spirals

Mandalas and spirals go together like peanut butter and jelly. Spirals symbolize growth, evolution, and the journey of life - and with the addition of the Fibonacci number sequence and the golden ratio, you've got a design that's out of this world!

With the spiral in your mandala, you can create a sense of flow, as if you are riding the waves of the universe itself. Spirals can also be used to represent the chakras, with each one leading to a different level of enlightenment. It's like your mandala is a map, guiding you through your spiritual journey.

The kundalini energy can also be represented with a spiral in your mandala. As the energy rises through the chakras, you're getting closer and closer to enlightenment - it's like a spiritual workout!

And let's not forget the DNA of each cell, which is shaped like a spiral double helix. With the spiral in your mandala, you're tapping into the intricate and awe-inspiring beauty of life itself.

So, the next time you're creating a mandala, don't be shy - add some spirals! Your design will not only look amazing, but it'll also have a deep spiritual significance that'll blow your mind. Get ready to spiral out into a world of creativity and enlightenment!

Choosing Colors and Symbols for Intentional Healing

Choosing Colors and Symbols for Intentional Healing

In the realm of intentional healing, colors, and symbols hold immense power. They have the ability to stir emotions, activate energies, and guide us on our healing journey. The art of selecting the right colors and symbols for healing purposes is an ancient practice that has been passed down through generations. Colors are the very fabric of light and hold secrets unseen by the naked eye. To ancient wisdom traditions, the wavelengths that captivate our senses carry healing frequencies that restore wholeness when body and spirit have fallen out of tune. By layering colors with intention, mandalas channel this spectral medicine, transmitting it as a balm for the soul.

Colors have long been associated with specific emotions and energies. Each color resonates with a different aspect of our being and has the power to influence our mood and state of mind. By consciously choosing colors that align with our intentions and desires, we can amplify the healing process and create a supportive environment for our soul's growth.

Consider for a moment the astonishing science within color. Every hue has its unique electromagnetic signature, measured in nanometers. When these wavelengths meet our eyes, they initiate a cascade of reactions. Like messengers, they inform the pineal gland to produce hormones that ripple throughout our systems, attuning our state of being.

But color's alchemy also works through subtler energetics. Mystics across traditions have mapped colors to energy centers called chakras that anchor our spiritual process. The deep red hue, for example, resonates with the pulsing life force located at the base of the spine. While cool, serene blues attune us to the heavens, opening a portal at the crown to our Divine essence.

The mandala brings all the aspects of color into synthesis. Its geometric form creates a crucible where the alchemical transformation unfolds. The placement of each hue has profound meaning. Colors anchored at the perimeter afford protection, containing the more vulnerable core. Radiant bursts of color within symbolize energies yearning for expression.

Like a time-release medicine, the longer we step into a mandala's spectrum of light, the deeper its healing unfolds. Layer by layer, it reveals to us where we need restoration and the luminous wholeness waiting to emerge when we allow our truth to blossom in its full-colored beauty.

Every color has its own unique vibe and significance, which means that the colors you choose in your mandala, can represent what your soul is seeking. For example, red is often associated with passion and energy, while blue represents calmness and tranquility.

And it is not just about the colors you use, but also how you use them. The placement of colors in a mandala can create a sense of balance and harmony or even a feeling of tension and conflict. Think about it:

a mandala with bright, bold colors arranged in a chaotic pattern might make you feel energized and excited, while a mandala with muted, earthy tones arranged in a more symmetrical pattern might make you feel calm and centered.

Colors are like chameleons; they can change their meaning depending on who is looking at them and what kind of day they are having. For example, red might make one person feel energized and passionate, while another person might associate it with anger and frustration. And don't even get me started on the green - some people see it as a symbol of growth and abundance, while others might associate it with envy and jealousy (hopefully not too much!).

But it's not just about personal preferences - colors can also have different meanings depending on the culture or context. In some cultures, white is a symbol of purity and innocence, while in others it's associated with death and mourning. Similarly, the color red can represent luck and prosperity in some Asian cultures, while in others it's considered a color of warning or danger.

Red

Oh, the fiery color red! It's like the spice in your favorite dish - it adds a little kick to everything. In mandalas, red is like the foundation, holding up the root chakra and keeping you grounded. Think of it like the roots of a tree - without them, the tree wouldn't be able to stand tall and strong.

In the world of spirituality, red is like a shot of espresso - it gives you energy and gets your heart pumping. It's the color of passion and desire, and it can help you feel more motivated and driven. Just be careful not to go overboard - too much red and you might start feeling like you're constantly running a marathon!

And in some cultures, red is like a lucky charm. It's like having a four-leaf clover in your pocket or finding a penny on the ground. In China, red is a symbol of good fortune and prosperity, so wearing red or incorporating it into your home decor might just bring you some luck.

So, whether you're looking to feel grounded, energized, or lucky, the color red has got you covered. Just remember to use it in moderation, unless you want to feel like you're sprinting through life all the time!"

Pink

The color of sweetness, tenderness, and pure loveliness! In the world of mandalas, pink is a crucial color that holds a special place.

Spiritually, pink is often linked to divine feminine and motherly love. It evokes feelings of tenderness, nurturing, and care. Pink is also associated with a sense of calmness and relaxation, making it an excellent color to use in meditation and spiritual practices. It can help to soothe the mind and connect us with the loving energy of the universe.

In some cultures, pink is also associated with innocence and youthfulness. In Japan, pink cherry blossoms are a symbol of renewal and the fleeting nature of life. They remind us to cherish each moment and to find beauty in impermanence.

So, let us embrace the power of pink! Whether you are looking to connect with your nurturing side, find a sense of peace and relaxation, or appreciate the beauty of life's fleeting moments, pink is the perfect color for you. Let's paint the town pink!

Yellow

Yellow - the color of sunshine, happiness, and the sun! That's right, yellow is a fun and playful color that brings joy and cheer to our lives.

In mandalas, yellow is an essential color that holds significant spiritual meaning.

In the world of chakras, yellow is associated with the solar plexus chakra, which is in the abdomen. This chakra represents our personal power, self-esteem, and confidence. When the solar plexus chakra is balanced, we feel strong, motivated, and self-assured. Using yellow in a mandala design can help activate and balance the solar plexus chakra, allowing us to tap into our inner strength and personal power.

In spiritual traditions, yellow is often associated with enlightenment and higher consciousness. It is a color that represents clarity of thought, mental agility, and spiritual awareness. In some cultures, yellow is also associated with royalty and nobility. In ancient Egypt, for example, yellow was the color of the pharaohs and was reserved for the highest members of society.

Whether you are looking to tap into your personal power, enhance your spiritual awareness, or just add a little sunshine to your life, Yellow has got you covered!

Orange

Ah, orange! The color of sunshine, joy, and citrus fruits. This bright and bold color is an important player in the world of mandalas, spirituality, and chakras.

In mandalas, orange is often associated with the sacral chakra, which is in the lower abdomen. This chakra represents creativity, passion, and pleasure. When the sacral chakra is balanced, we can tap into our inner creative juices and feel more connected to our desires and passions. Using orange in a mandala design can help to activate and balance the sacral chakra, allowing us to embrace our inner artists and tap into our creative potential.

In spiritual traditions, orange is often associated with joy and enthusiasm. It is a color that can help to uplift our spirits and bring a sense of positivity into our lives. Orange is also associated with generosity and giving, making it a great color to use when we want to express our gratitude and show appreciation to others.

In some cultures, orange is also associated with celebration and good luck. In India, for example, orange is a sacred color and is often associated with the Hindu god Brahma. During the festival of Holi, people throw colored powders, including orange, at each other in celebration of spring and good fortune.

Whether you are looking to tap into your creative side, add some joy and positivity to your life, or celebrate a special occasion, the color orange might just be the perfect color for you!

Green

Green is the superhero of the chakra world, fighting for love and harmony with its trusty sidekick, the heart chakra. Together, they form an unbeatable team that promotes balance, connection, and all things warm and fuzzy.

In mandalas, green is the go-to color for the heart chakra, bringing a sense of calm and tranquility to your design. It's like a big, green hug from Mother Nature herself!

Just like the new leaves on a spring day, green represents fresh starts and new beginnings. It's a reminder that even in the darkest of times, there's always hope for growth and change.

But green is not just a chakra superhero - it's also a symbol of growth and renewal, making it the ultimate life coach. Want to sprout some new ideas or take on a new project? Greens got your back.

Therefore, if you want to tap into the power of love, growth, and balance, go green and let your mandala design shine!

Blue

Blue - the color of the sky, the ocean, and those little pills that help you calm down! Blue is a popular color in many cultures and holds significant spiritual meaning in the world of mandalas and chakras.

In mandalas, blue is often associated with the throat chakra, which is located in the neck area. The throat chakra represents communication and self-expression, and it is associated with feelings of honesty, truthfulness, and clarity. When the throat chakra is balanced, we can communicate our thoughts and feelings clearly and effectively. Using blue in a mandala design can help activate and balance the throat chakra, allowing us to speak our truth and communicate effectively.

In spiritual traditions, blue is often associated with wisdom and spiritual insight. It is a color that represents calmness, clarity, and inner peace. Blue is also associated with the divine, representing the vastness and mystery of the universe.

In some cultures, blue is also associated with protection and good luck. In many Middle Eastern countries, for example, blue evil eye beads are believed to ward off negative energy and protect against the evil eye.

So, whether you're looking to communicate more effectively, tap into your spiritual wisdom, or protect yourself from negative energy, blue might just be the color for you!

Purple

Oh, purple, the majestic color of royalty, spirituality, and magic! It's no wonder this color has a special place in the world of mandalas.

In spiritual traditions, purple is often associated with enlightenment and spiritual awareness. It is believed to help open the third eye chakra, which is located between the eyebrows and is associated with intuition, insight, and inner wisdom. Using purple in a mandala design can help to activate and balance the third eye chakra, allowing us to tap into our inner wisdom and see the world with a clearer perspective.

Purple is also associated with creativity, imagination, and magic. It is a color that inspires us to think outside the box and tap into our deepest desires. In some cultures, purple is also associated with wealth and luxury, as it was once a rare and expensive color to produce.

So, whether you are seeking spiritual enlightenment, tapping into your creative side, or just looking to add a touch of magic to your life, incorporating purple into your mandala design is sure to bring a touch of enchantment to your journey. Let's paint the town purple!

So next time you're choosing colors for creating a mandala or just picking out an outfit for the day, remember that the meanings behind colors are more complex than meets the eye. In addition, if someone tells you that you cannot wear green because it clashes with your skin tone, just tell him or her you are channeling your inner Hulk and go rock that emerald, green!

Consider the colors you are using and how they are arranged. You might just be surprised at how much of an impact they can have on your mood and well-being.

Indigo

Indigo, oh the color that is like a mysterious midnight sky, filled with stars and secrets waiting to be uncovered! It is a blend of dark blue and red, like a cosmic cocktail of depth and intensity. In the world of mandalas, indigo holds a special place, making the connection between the physical and spiritual worlds even stronger.

Indigo is the color associated with the third eye chakra, nestled right in the center of the forehead. This chakra is like a cosmic third eye that connects us to our intuition, insight, and inner wisdom. When the third eye chakra is balanced, our sixth sense is heightened, allowing us to tap into our intuition and connect with the universe in new and exciting ways.

Using indigo in your mandala design is like giving your third eye a cosmic caffeine boost. It helps activate and balance this important chakra, enhancing your self-awareness, and inspiring deeper reflection. The result? A meditative and reflective space that helps you unlock your innermost thoughts and feelings.

In addition to its chakra associations, indigo is also associated with wisdom and higher learning. In ancient times, indigo was used by priests and priestesses in their clothing to symbolize their spiritual knowledge and connection to the divine.

Therefore, whether you are looking to unlock your inner wisdom or add a cosmic touch to your mandala designs, indigo is the perfect color to help you on your spiritual journey!

Grey

Grey, the color that is not quite black and not quite white, but somewhere in between! While it may not seem like the most exciting color at first glance, grey actually holds a lot of significance in the world of mandalas.

Grey is often used in mandalas to represent balance and neutrality. It can help to create a calming and grounding energy, allowing us to connect with our inner selves and find a sense of peace.

Incorporating grey into a mandala design can also help to bring clarity and focus to our thoughts. It is like a blank canvas that allows us to create our own meaning and interpretation. This makes the link between the world and our soul clearer, inspiring reflection and self-awareness.

Grey is also a color that is associated with resilience and adaptability. It is a reminder that life is not always black and white, but that we can find strength and balance even in the grey areas.

So, do not underestimate the power of grey in your mandala designs! It may not be the flashiest color, but it can help you to create a harmonious and balanced spiritual journey.

Black

Oh, the mysterious and alluring color black! Some may say that black is the absence of color, but to me, it is like a blank canvas just waiting to be transformed into a masterpiece.

In the world of mandalas, black is a powerful color that can be used to represent the unknown, the mysterious, and the hidden. It can also symbolize strength, protection, and grounding. Incorporating black into a mandala design can help you connect with your innermost thoughts and feelings and bring a sense of balance and stability to your life.

Black is like a magician's cape, hiding secrets and mysteries just waiting to be discovered. It is like the night sky, filled with twinkling stars and infinite possibilities. Using black in a mandala can help you tap into your intuition and unleash your creative powers, allowing you to explore the depths of your soul and connect with the universe on a deeper level.

So, if you are feeling lost or overwhelmed, or if you are simply looking to add a touch of mystery and intrigue to your mandala designs, do not forget the power of black! Let it guide you on a journey of self-discovery and inner exploration.

White

"White, oh sweet simplicity! It is the color of purity, clarity, and illumination in the mystical world of mandalas and spirituality. Think of it as a blank canvas, the potential for new beginnings and endless possibilities. White also represents peace and serenity, providing a soothing and tranquil space for meditation and self-reflection.

In some cultures, white is revered as a sacred color, signifying the connection between heaven and earth, the divine and the human. Angels ascended masters, and other enlightened beings are often depicted wearing white.

Using white in your mandala designs can create a sense of spaciousness, allowing your mind to wander freely and explore new ideas and perspectives. It can also create balance and harmony, promoting a sense of well-being and inner peace.

So, if you are ready to embark on a spiritual journey, do not be afraid to add some white to your mandala designs. It just might be the perfect color to help you tap into your highest potential and connect with the divine."

Brown

Ah, the color of rich soil and steaming hot chocolate! Brown is a vital color in the world of mandalas and spirituality, representing stability, grounding, and the earth element. It is like a warm hug from Mother Nature, reminding us to stay connected to the physical world and providing a strong foundation for spiritual growth.

In mandalas, brown can be used to promote a sense of security and balance, providing comforting and supportive energy. It can also remind us of the importance of taking care of ourselves, just like the earth needs nourishment and care to thrive.

Using brown in a mandala design can help to deepen our connection to the natural world and the cycles of life, encouraging us to live in harmony with the planet and all its inhabitants. So, whether you are seeking stability, comfort, or a deeper connection to the earth, do not forget the power of brown in your sacred mandala designs!

Silver

Silver, the mysterious and enchanting color of the moon, and intuition! When it comes to creating a sacred mandala, silver can hold great significance. It is often used to represent the feminine energy, as well as the subconscious mind and the spiritual realm.

Silver is a color of reflection, clarity, and purity, offering a mirror-like surface to see ourselves and the world around us with fresh eyes. It helps us to tune into our intuition and connect with our higher selves, encouraging us to explore the unknown and the unseen with an open heart and mind.

In mandalas, silver can add a touch of mystery and depth, evoking a sense of otherworldliness and spirituality. Its subtle shimmer and shine can help to create a soothing and calming atmosphere, inviting us to explore our innermost thoughts and emotions.

So, whether you are seeking to connect with your intuitive side or simply looking to add a touch of mystery and magic to your mandala, silver is a powerful and versatile color to incorporate into your design.

Gold

Gold - the color of the sun, strength, and prosperity! This radiant hue is often linked to the divine masculine and abundance, encouraging us to connect with our higher selves and live life to the fullest.

Gold is also a symbol of power and confidence, reminding us to embrace our own strength and inner radiance.

In mandalas, gold can create a feeling of luxury and opulence, inviting us to explore the fullness and richness of life. It's warm and glowing nature can inspire us to tap into our own inner light and shine as brightly as the sun. So, when designing your next mandala, do not forget to include a touch of golden magic to ignite your inner radiance!

Similarly, symbols hold deep meaning and carry the wisdom of ancient traditions. They act as gateways to the subconscious mind, unlocking hidden knowledge and guiding us toward our true purpose. Each symbol holds a unique vibration and can be utilized to awaken specific energies within us. By carefully selecting symbols that resonate with our personal journey, we can tap into their transformative power and facilitate healing on a deep level.

Sacred mandalas offer a profound healing journey for the soul. These intricate geometric designs combine both colors and symbols in a harmonious way, creating a visual representation of our inner world. By meditating on these mandalas, we can access the deeper layers of our consciousness and gain insights into our own healing process. The colors and symbols within the mandala act as catalysts, guiding us toward our true essence and facilitating the release of stagnant energies.

In conclusion, choosing the right colors and symbols for intentional healing is a powerful practice that can deeply impact our soul's vibration. By aligning ourselves with the energies and intentions represented by specific colors and symbols, we can accelerate our healing journey and awaken our true potential. Sacred mandalas serve as a transformative tool, inviting us to explore the depths of our being and facilitating profound healing and transformation. As we delve into the world of colors and symbols, we embark on a sacred journey toward self-discovery and alignment with our soul's vibration.

Chapter 5

Sacred Mandalas for Transformation

Mandala Meditations for Self-Reflection and Growth

Mandala Meditations for Self-Reflection and Growth

In our fast-paced and chaotic world, it is easy to lose touch with our inner selves and the deep wisdom that resides within us. However, there is a powerful tool that can help us reconnect with our true essence and embark on a profound healing journey for our soul – the sacred mandala.

Mandalas have been used for centuries by various cultures as a spiritual and creative practice. Derived from the Sanskrit word for "circle," mandalas represent wholeness, unity, and the interconnectedness of all things. They serve as a visual representation of our inner world, allowing us to explore and understand the depths of our psyche.

Within the pages of this subchapter, you will find a rich collection of mandalas that I have created, and meditations designed to guide you through the process of self-reflection and growth. These meditations will help you uncover the hidden aspects of your being, release emotional blockages, and tap into your innate healing abilities.

Each mandala meditation is carefully crafted to address different facets of your soul's journey. Whether you are seeking clarity, emotional healing, or spiritual transformation, there is a meditation that will resonate with your unique needs. Through the practice of mandala meditations, you will learn to cultivate mindfulness, connect with your intuition, and embrace your soul's true purpose.

As you immerse yourself in the sacred realm of mandala meditations, you will discover the profound healing and transformation that can occur when you align with your soul's vibration. These meditative practices will empower you to release old patterns, embrace your authentic self, and live a life filled with purpose and joy.

Benefits of Meditating on a Sacred Mandala

Meditating on a mandala is a sacred journey that holds incredible benefits for your mind, body, and spirit. Let us explore the wondrous advantages of diving into the depths of a mandala meditation:

Serenity and Relaxation: Gazing upon the intricate patterns and symmetrical designs of a mandala can instantly transport you to a state of tranquility. As you immerse yourself in its beauty, the mind begins to quiet, and a deep sense of calm washes over you. It is like entering a peaceful sanctuary where worries and stress melt away.

Mindfulness and Presence: The mandala serves as an anchor for your attention, guiding you into the present moment. With each breath, you become fully aware of the intricate details and vibrant colors. Your focus becomes laser-sharp, and the incessant chatter of the mind begins to fade. In this state of mindfulness, you experience a heightened sense of clarity and inner peace.

Deep Self-Reflection: The mandala acts as a mirror, reflecting the inner landscape of your being. As you contemplate its patterns, colors, and symbols, you embark on a journey of self-discovery. You may uncover hidden emotions, gain insights into your thoughts and beliefs, and awaken dormant aspects of your true self. It becomes a gateway to exploring your innermost desires, fears, and aspirations.

Emotional Healing: The mandala possesses a unique ability to heal and balance your emotions. As you engage with its harmonious shapes and colors, you invite emotional energy to flow and release. It provides a safe space for exploring and processing complex feelings, offering solace and comfort during challenging times. Through this process, you gain emotional resilience and a renewed sense of inner harmony.

Enhanced Creativity: The mandala is a wellspring of creative inspiration. By engaging with its artistic expression, you awaken the dormant artist within you. It stimulates your imagination, ignites innovative thinking, and unlocks new perspectives. As you delve into the creative realm of the mandala, you open doors to limitless possibilities and unlock your innate creative potential.

Spiritual Connection: Within the sacred geometry of the mandala, you can deepen your spiritual connection. It serves as a portal to higher realms, inviting divine energy and wisdom to flow through you. By immersing yourself in its intricate patterns, you can experience a sense of oneness with the universe, tapping into your spiritual essence and expanding your consciousness.

Stress Reduction and Well-being: The practice of mandala meditation has profound effects on your overall well-being. As you engage in this mindful activity, stress levels diminish, tension is released, and a state of inner balance is restored. The positive energy generated by the mandala infuses your entire being, promoting physical, emotional, and mental harmony.

Remember, the true beauty of meditating on a mandala lies in your personal experience. Each journey is unique, unveiling its own treasures and insights. So, allow yourself to embark on this transformative adventure and let the mandala guide you to new realms of self-discovery, healing, and spiritual growth.

Guided meditation script that focuses on a mandala:

Begin by finding a quiet, comfortable place to sit. Take a few deep breaths and allow yourself to relax.

Recall a mandala that speaks to you. It might be a mandala that you have created yourself, or it might be a mandala that you have seen somewhere else. Allow the image of the mandala to come into focus in your mind's eye.

As you gaze at the mandala, allow yourself to become absorbed in its beauty and complexity. Notice the colors, the shapes, and the patterns. Allow yourself to be drawn into the center of the mandala, where you may find a sense of peace and calm.

As you continue to focus on the mandala, allow yourself to let go of any thoughts or worries that may be on your mind. Simply be present with the mandala and allow yourself to be in the moment.

As you continue to gaze at the mandala, you may find that your mind begins to quiet. Allow yourself to simply be with the mandala and allow yourself to be at peace.

When you feel ready, slowly begin to bring your attention back to your surroundings. Take a few deep breaths and allow yourself to return to the present moment. When you feel ready, gently open your eyes.

Remember, this is your own personal meditation, so feel free to adapt the script to your own needs and preferences. The most important thing is to find a sense of calm and peace within yourself as you focus on the mandala.

Visualize elements within the design. Take a moment to explore these symbols and allow yourself to connect with their meanings.

As you gaze at the mandala, imagine that you are being drawn into its center. As you enter the center, you may find yourself in a peaceful, calm space. Spend a few moments here, allowing yourself to be at peace and in the present moment.

Imagine that you can step into the mandala and become part of the design. As you walk through the mandala, you may find that you are drawn to certain symbols or elements. Take a moment to explore these symbols and allow yourself to connect with their meanings.

As you focus on the mandala, imagine that it is a window into another world or dimension. As you gaze into the mandala, allow yourself to be open to any insights or messages that may come to you.

The Relaxing Mandala Meditation:

Begin by finding a quiet and comfortable place where you can sit or lie down undisturbed. Get into a comfortable position, whether it is sitting cross-legged on the floor, sitting in a chair with your feet firmly on the ground, or lying down on a mat or blanket. Close your eyes and take a moment to focus on your breath.

Take deep breaths in through your nose and out through your mouth, allowing yourself to feel the rise and fall of your chest with each inhalation and exhalation. As you focus on your breathing, allow your mind to quiet and your body to relax.

Visualize a beautiful, calming mandala in front of you. The mandala can be any color or shape that appeals to you but imagine it as a radiant, glowing object that fills your mind with serenity and peace. As you gaze upon the mandala, allow its colors and shapes to fill your mind and calm your body.

Focus on each color and shape, one at a time, and let them guide you into a state of relaxation. Pay attention to the way each color and shape makes you feel, and let those feelings sink into your body. Perhaps the blue color in the mandala makes you feel calm, or the red shape evokes a feeling of warmth. Allow yourself to sink into these feelings and let them permeate your entire being.

Stay in this relaxed state for as long as you like. When you are ready, take a deep breath and slowly open your eyes, feeling refreshed and renewed. This meditation can be done for a few minutes or for a longer period of time, depending on your needs and preferences. The goal is to find peace and relaxation through the visualization of the mandala.

The Root Chakra Mandala guided meditation.

Find a comfortable seated position and gently close your eyes. Take a deep breath in through your nose, feeling your belly expand, and exhale through your mouth, feeling your whole body relax.

Visualize yourself standing in a beautiful garden, surrounded by tall trees and colorful flowers. In the center of the garden is a mandala with earthy brown colors, representing the root chakra. As you approach the mandala, you feel a sense of being grounded and stability washing over you.

Now, let's use positive affirmations to tap into the power of the Root Chakra. Repeat the following affirmations to yourself, starting with "I am":

- I am rooted, I am grounded, I am safe.
- I am rooted and grounded in the present moment.
- I am worthy and deserving of abundance in all areas of my life.
- I am safe and secure, and all my needs are met with ease.
- I am strong and resilient, able to overcome any obstacles.
- I am connected to the earth and its healing energy.
- I am balanced and harmonious in my body, mind, and spirit.

Visualize your roots growing deep into the earth, connecting you to the earth's energy and stability.

As you focus on the mandala, notice the intricate patterns and shapes within it. Allow yourself to get lost in the design, feeling a sense of calm and serenity. Repeat to yourself, "I am present, I am centered, I am calm."

Take a deep breath in and exhale any tension or stress you may be holding in your body. Allow yourself to fully surrender to the present moment and the peaceful energy of the mandala.

When you are ready, gently open your eyes and take a moment to notice how you feel. Take this feeling of rootedness and calm with you as you continue with your day. Remember that you are always connected to the earth's energy, and you are safe and grounded in every moment.

The Sacral Chakra Mandala Meditation

As you begin to relax, take a deep breath, and close your eyes. Visualize yourself in a peaceful place, surrounded by warm, orange light.

As you breathe in, imagine this warm orange light filling your body with a sense of warmth and relaxation. As you breathe out, release any tension you may be holding onto, and feel yourself sinking deeper into a state of relaxation.

Now, let's bring our attention to the sacral chakra, located in your lower abdomen. This energy center governs our emotions, creativity, and sexuality.

Visualize a beautiful mandala featuring shades of orange, the color of the sacral chakra. See it growing and expanding, filling your entire body with its warmth and energy.

Now, let's use positive affirmations to tap into the power of the sacral chakra. Repeat the following affirmations to yourself, starting with "I feel":

- I feel deeply connected to my emotions.
- I feel inspired and creative.
- I feel comfortable expressing my sexuality.
- I feel a sense of joy and passion in all aspects of my life.
- I feel balanced and in harmony with my emotions.

As you repeat these affirmations, feel the energy of the sacral chakra growing stronger within you. See the mandala growing brighter and more vibrant, reflecting your inner power and creativity.

Take a few deep breaths, and when you're ready, slowly open your eyes, feeling refreshed and energized. Remember, you have the power within you to tap into your emotions and creativity, and to express your true self with confidence and joy.

The Solar Plexus Mandala Meditation

Welcome to a transformative meditation journey that will empower your solar plexus chakra, the radiant center of your personal power and self-confidence. Find a comfortable position, close your eyes, and let's embark on this vibrant meditation with the radiant energy of the mandala.

As you settle into a calm state, envision a mandala before you, glowing with vibrant shades of yellow, radiating warmth and strength. Let its energy envelop you, awakening your solar plexus chakra and igniting your inner fire.

Take a deep breath in, and as you exhale, repeat the positive affirmation, "I do possess immense personal power within me." Feel the resonance of these words within your being, as they awaken your inner strength and self-assurance.

Imagine a golden light emanating from the mandala, gently flowing into your solar plexus area. With each inhale, this luminous energy expands and intensifies, infusing you with confidence and vitality. As you exhale, release any doubts or insecurities that have held you back.

With every breath, visualize the mandala's intricate patterns and bold shapes resonating with your personal power. Feel it growing stronger within you, igniting a fiery energy that fuels your ambitions and fuels your actions.

Repeat the affirmation, "I do embrace my personal power fearlessly." Feel the words reverberate through your entire being, empowering you to step into your greatness and embrace your authentic self.

Allow the mandala's energy to swirl and dance within your solar plexus, clearing away any blocks or limitations that hinder your self-confidence. Visualize any stagnant energy dissolving, making space for a vibrant and magnetic aura.

Now, take a moment to reflect on a recent achievement or success that you're proud of. As you hold this accomplishment in your mind, affirm, "I do celebrate my accomplishments and acknowledge my worth." Feel the warmth of validation and self-appreciation fill your being.

As the meditation draws to a close, express gratitude to the mandala for its healing energy and affirm, "I do radiate confidence and personal power in all areas of my life."

Gently bring your awareness back to the present moment, carrying the empowering energy of the solar plexus chakra with you. Remember, you hold the power to manifest your dreams and embrace your true potential.

Whenever you need a boost of confidence or a reminder of your inner strength, return to this meditation, and let the mandala and affirmations reignite your personal power. Embrace your journey of empowerment and continue to shine brightly in all that you do.

The Heart Chakra Mandala Meditation

Welcome to a serene meditation experience centered around the heart chakra, the radiant energy of love and compassion. Find a comfortable position, close your eyes, and let us embark on this journey of heart-centered relaxation with the healing power of the mandala.

Imagine a gentle, emerald-green mandala before you, emanating soothing vibrations of love and harmony. As you focus on its intricate patterns and calming hues, feel your heart center opening and expanding, inviting in love, compassion, and connection.

Take a deep breath in, and as you exhale, repeat the positive affirmation, "I love and accept myself unconditionally." Feel the warmth and tenderness of these words embracing your entire being, as you cultivate a deep sense of self-love and acceptance.

Envision the green light of the mandala radiating outward, infusing your heart chakra with its healing energy. With each breath, feel your heart center blossoming like a beautiful flower, releasing any pain or emotional burdens that no longer serve you.

As you continue to breathe deeply, let the love within you expand beyond your physical body, reaching out to embrace all beings and the world around you. Visualize the interconnectedness of all living things and feel a sense of unity and compassion filling your heart.

Repeat the affirmation, "I love and honor all beings with an open heart." Allow these words to resonate within you, as you tap into the infinite well of love within your being and extend it to others.

Imagine the green light of the mandala flowing through every cell of your body, revitalizing, and harmonizing your energy. Feel any tension or emotional blockages dissolve, making way for a profound sense of peace and love.

With each breath, imagine the mandala's gentle energy circulating in your heart space, healing any past hurts, and nurturing forgiveness. Visualize any emotional wounds being bathed in the soothing green light, transforming into pure love and compassion.

As the meditation nears its end, express gratitude to the mandala for its healing energy and affirm, "I love and am loved unconditionally." Feel the profound truth of these words permeating your entire being, as you embody the essence of love and become a beacon of compassion.

Gently bring your awareness back to the present moment, carrying the loving energy of the heart chakra with you. Remember, love is the guiding force in your life, and by nurturing and sharing it, you create a ripple effect of healing and harmony.

Whenever you seek solace, connection, or a reminder of the boundless love within you, return to this meditation, and let the mandala and affirmations guide you back to the loving essence of your heart. Embrace the power of love, and let it radiate in every facet of your existence.

The Throat Chakra Mandala Mediation

Find a comfortable and peaceful space where you can immerse yourself in this guided meditation. Begin by taking a few deep and calming breaths, allowing your body to relax and your mind to let go of any tension.

As you close your eyes, visualize a gentle blue light enveloping your throat area. This is the radiant energy of the throat chakra, the center of communication, self-expression, and authenticity. Feel this soothing blue light expanding with every breath, clearing any blockages and creating a harmonious flow of energy.

Imagine before you a mandala, its intricate patterns swirling with shades of blue and light. This mandala is your gateway to the realm of the throat chakra, a space where your true voice can resonate and be heard.

Gently gaze upon the mandala, allowing its beauty to captivate you. As you do, let these positive affirmations weave through your thoughts:

"I express myself authentically, for my voice is a unique gift."

"My words hold power, and I use them to create positive change."

"I trust in my ability to communicate with clarity and confidence."

"I am aligned with my inner truth, and I share it with the world."

"I embrace my creative expression and let my voice flow freely."

Feel the energy of your throat chakra responding to each affirmation, like a river of soothing blue light expanding and resonating within you. As you continue to focus on the mandala, allow any thoughts, feelings, or messages related to self-expression and communication to surface.

With each breath, you are opening the channels of your throat chakra, allowing your true voice to flow effortlessly. As you sit in this tranquil state, imagine yourself confidently expressing your thoughts, ideas, and feelings with authenticity and ease.

As the meditation comes to a close, gently bring your awareness back to your breath, feeling the rise and fall of your chest. Carry the empowered energy of your throat chakra with you as you open your eyes, ready to communicate with authenticity and grace in your daily life.

Remember, your voice matters, and through the magic of this meditation, you have tapped into the energy of the throat chakra, your gateway to self-expression and clear communication.

The Third Eye Chakra Mandala meditation

As you prepare to embark on this journey within, take a moment to find a comfortable and peaceful space where you can fully immerse yourself. Let your body settle into a relaxed position, allowing your breath to flow effortlessly, like a gentle rhythm of life itself.

As you close your eyes, envision a canvas of darkness, a blank slate for your inner exploration. Now, visualize a radiant mandala, its intricate patterns and vibrant colors beginning to form before you. This mandala is your portal to the realm of the third eye chakra, a center of intuition, insight, and inner wisdom.

Gaze upon the mandala with a sense of wonder, letting its energy draw you in. As you look at its mesmerizing patterns, imagine a soothing indigo light surrounding you, gently activating your third eye chakra. Feel this indigo light expanding, illuminating your inner vision and awakening the dormant insights that lie within.

In this space of heightened awareness, let's weave positive affirmations into your journey:

"I trust my intuition, for it is my compass on this journey of life."

"I am open to receiving divine insights that guide me on my path."

"I see beyond the surface, tapping into the wisdom of my higher self."

"I embrace the mysteries of the universe, knowing that all answers reside within."

"I am connected to the infinite wisdom of the cosmos, and it flows through me effortlessly."

With each affirmation, feel the energy of your third eye chakra growing stronger, like a beacon of light piercing through the darkness. As you continue to gaze at the mandala, allow any images, messages, or sensations to arise naturally. Trust your inner knowing, and let it guide you through this sacred exploration.

As your meditation comes to a close, gently bring your awareness back to your breath, back to the present moment. Carry the insights and wisdom you have gained from this experience with you, knowing that you can tap into your third eye chakra's guidance whenever you need.

With gratitude and newfound clarity, slowly open your eyes, embracing the world around you with a deeper understanding of your inner wisdom.

The Crown Chakra Mandala meditation

Find a comfortable seat and close your eyes. Take a deep breath in through your nose and out through your mouth. Feel your body relaxing with each inhale and exhale. Set your intention to connect to the divine wisdom within you.

Bring your awareness to the crown of your head. Visualize a beautiful mandala or sacred geometry spinning lightly above you. Its intricate patterns and designs glow with violet light.

The mandala represents your connection to universal consciousness and divine wisdom. As you observe its hypnotic movement, feelings of peace and tranquility flow down from its violet light into your crown chakra. Just like this balanced artwork, you are intricately connected to the wholeness of the universe.

With each breath, feel the area around your crown chakra becoming more open and relaxed. Any tension you are holding in your head or neck begins to dissolve.

You are tapping into infinite inspiration, imagination, and spiritual intuition. New ideas and insights arise effortlessly. You are realigning to your highest purpose.

Continue observing the spinning mandala above your head. With each rotation, it clears and cleanses your crown chakra. Negative thoughts drop away. Divine guidance and understanding fill you completely. Repeat the following: I am one with the Divine, the Divine loves me" Fill every cell with that powerful affirmation.

You are now fully connected to your higher self and the infinite well of wisdom within you. You are guided by an inner knowledge far beyond your normal conscious mind.

Take a moment to recite I am connected to the universe. Feel your relationship to all of existence. You are a thread in its grand tapestry, important to the overall design.

Now picture at the center of the mandala a sparkling light, representing your higher self. This is your inner wisdom, your true essence. This light has always been inside you, guiding you. Focus on the light and repeat: I am true to my divine path. Your higher self knows the way. Stay committed to following its radiance.

See the light at your core expand outward until it merges with the rest of the mandala. Realize that your higher self is one with the universe. Say: I am one with my higher self. You are never separated from your inner wisdom. It lives within you and surrounds you.

When you feel ready, take a deep breath, and open your eyes, feeling energized and connected. Carry this expanded sense of intuition and creativity into your daily life. Remember, you have unlimited access to inner wisdom and are always divinely guided. Trust that you are on the right path.

Mandalas for Chakra Healing and Balancing

Mandalas for Chakra Healing and Balancing

As we embark on our journey towards healing and transformation, understanding the power of sacred mandalas can be a guiding light, leading us towards aligning our soul's vibration.

Mandalas, ancient geometric symbols, have been used for centuries as tools for meditation, self-reflection, and healing. Each mandala is a unique creation, containing intricate patterns and colors that resonate with specific energies and frequencies. These energies can be harnessed to heal and balance our chakra system, the subtle energy centers within our bodies.

Our chakra system consists of seven main energy centers, which govern different aspects of our physical, emotional, and spiritual well-being. When these energy centers become blocked or imbalanced, it can manifest as various physical or emotional ailments. Sacred mandalas offer a pathway to harmonize and restore the flow of energy within these chakras, facilitating healing on multiple levels.

By working with specific mandalas designed for each chakra, we can engage in a deep and transformative healing journey for the soul. Each mandala is infused with the energetic qualities required to bring balance and alignment to a particular chakra. Through focused meditation, visualization, and contemplation, we can activate and purify these energy centers, promoting overall well-being and spiritual growth. By engaging with these mandalas, we can activate and cultivate the qualities associated with each chakra, facilitating a profound healing experience.

The Marvelous Mandala: A Cosmic Coloring Book

Imagine you are holding a mystical coloring book, one filled with intricate patterns that seem to come alive as you touch them. These patterns, dear reader, are the sacred mandalas; cosmic blueprints that can help us align our chakras and bring harmony to our very existence. It is like spiritual therapy for the artist within you. And just like choosing the perfect color for your masterpiece, selecting the right mandala to work with is a delightful adventure.

Chakras: The Energetic Spin Doctors

Now, let's chat about those famous energy hubs known as chakras. Picture them as your personal spiritual DJs, spinning energy records that harmonize your mind, body, and spirit. Sometimes, these DJs need a little tune-up, a bit like fixing a hiccup in your favorite song. Enter the mandalas – our cosmic mechanics that can get your chakras grooving in perfect harmony.

Rooting for the Root Chakra: Getting Grounded with Mandalas

The first stop is the root chakra – our foundational energy center. It is like the concrete slab that keeps your spiritual house from floating away in a cosmic breeze. Feeling jittery, scared, anxious and unbalanced? Time to tap into the grounding vibes of a mandala. Imagine you are planting your feet on solid mandala ground, like your very own superhero stance. Choose earthy colors and intricate geometric patterns to anchor your root chakra and find stability in a wobbly world. As you draw, imagine roots extending from your spine, connecting you to the earth. This will make you feel supported and unshakable.

Sacral Safari: Mandalas for Creative Flow

Ready for the sacral chakra adventure? This energy center's all about the creative flow – that artistic river coursing through you. This chakra is your creative powerhouse, your passion, and your sensuality. Mandalas can be your creativity booster, unleashing an artistic floodgate of ideas. Picture yourself dipping your paintbrush into the pool of mandala energy, letting its vibrant hues infuse your creative endeavors. Let your design be free-flowing and dynamic, with swirling shapes and curves. As you draw, tap into your creative energy, allowing it to flow freely. This will awaken your inspiration, your passion, and your zest for life.

Solar Plexus Power-Up: Boosting Confidence with Mandalas

Ah, the solar plexus chakra, where confidence and willpower reside. Think of it as your inner cheerleader, the one that roots for you when life throws curveballs. Grab a mandala that resonates with your warrior spirit – bold lines, fiery colors – and let it empower your sense of self. Imagine your solar plexus chakra soaking up this potent energy, fueling your inner fire like a cosmic power-up. Feel yourself becoming stronger, more confident, and more in control - like a true superhero!

Heartfelt Mandalas: Where Love and Healing Meet

The heart chakra is the bridge between earthly and divine love. It represents your ability to give and receive love, compassion, and connection - the stuff that makes life magical. Time for some mandala magic that taps into the very essence of compassion and healing. Choose gentle, soothing colors that evoke feelings of love and connection. Gaze upon your heart-centered mandala, and imagine it radiating waves of love and kindness, like cosmic heartbeats, spreading love to every corner of your being.

Throat Chakra: Speak Your Truth with Mandala Confidence

Feeling tongue-tied? It's your throat chakra – your truth speaker – asking for the spotlight. Mandalas can be your speech coach, helping you articulate your thoughts with grace. Focus on creating a design that feels clear and concise, with sharp and defined lines and shapes Visualize your throat chakra expanding and spinning like a mandala, gaining the confidence to express yourself authentically. Remember, our words have a vibration that can heal or destroy.

Third Eye Awakens: Mandalas for Intuition

Ah, the third eye chakra, where intuition and insight reside. It's like your cosmic radar, guiding you through the mysteries of life. Allow a mandala to be your intuitive compass. As you meditate on its intricate patterns, feel your third eye awakening, granting you a deeper connection to your inner wisdom. Trust your intuition, for it's the universe's way of whispering guidance.

Crowning Glory: Mandalas for Spiritual Connection

Last but certainly not least, the crown chakra – our gateway to the divine, your higher self, and your spiritual purpose. Think of it as your spiritual Wi-Fi, connecting you to higher realms. Mandalas can be your antennas, tuning you into this cosmic channel. Choose mandalas with ethereal patterns and shades, like starlit skies, as you visualize your crown chakra blossoming like a lotus flower. The heart and mind can find their common ground in the infinity of a moment.

In Conclusion: Unveiling the Masterpiece Within

Furthermore, the practice of creating our own mandalas can be a powerful tool for self-expression and personal growth. As we engage in this creative process, we tap into our innate wisdom and intuition, allowing our soul's vibration to guide us. The act of coloring or drawing mandalas can be a meditative practice, helping us quiet the mind and connect with our higher selves.

In this dance of chakras and mandalas, you're the artist and the canvas, the masterpiece, and the creator. As you explore the world of sacred mandalas for chakra healing and balancing, you are stepping onto a cosmic stage where colors, patterns, and energies unite to unveil the radiant masterpiece that is YOU.

By engaging with specific mandalas for each chakra, we can activate, purify, and harmonize these energy centers, promoting holistic well-being. Additionally, the practice of creating our own mandalas can be a deeply meditative and introspective process, fostering personal growth and self-discovery. Embrace the healing power of mandalas and embark on a sacred journey toward awakening your soul's vibration.

Using Mandalas for Manifestation and Goal Setting

Using Mandalas for Manifestation and Goal Setting

In the sacred journey of healing and transformation, mandalas have long been revered as powerful tools. These intricate and symmetrical designs can tap into the deepest recesses of our souls, allowing us to connect with our innermost desires and aspirations. For those in need of healing and seeking to follow their soul vibration, sacred mandalas can serve as guides, facilitating the manifestation of goals and dreams.

Manifestation is the process of bringing our desires into reality through intention and focused energy. By using mandalas as a visual representation of our goals, we can harness their profound energy and direct it toward our desired outcomes. The geometric patterns and vibrant colors of the mandalas act as catalysts for transformation, amplifying our intentions and helping to align our energies with the universe.

To begin using mandalas for manifestation and goal setting, it is important to first identify your intentions and desires. Take some time to reflect on what you truly want to manifest in your life – whether it is physical, emotional, or spiritual healing or the achievement of specific goals and dreams. Once you have clarity on your intentions, find or create a mandala that resonates with you and represents your desired outcome.

Engaging with the mandala is a meditative practice that involves focusing your attention on its intricate details and allowing yourself to become immersed in its energy. You can do this by simply gazing at the mandala, tracing its patterns with your finger, or even coloring it in. As you connect with the mandala, visualize your desired outcome, and infuse it with positive emotions and feelings. Imagine yourself already living the life you desire, experiencing the healing and transformation you seek.

By consistently engaging with your chosen mandala and maintaining a strong connection to your intentions, you can begin to witness the manifestation process unfold. The energy you invest in the mandala will attract similar energies from the universe, creating a powerful synergy that supports the realization of your goals. Remember to trust the process and remain open to receiving guidance and opportunities that align with your intentions.

Using mandalas for manifestation and goal setting is a sacred and transformative journey. As you delve deeper into this practice, you will discover the immense power that lies within yourself to heal, transform, and manifest your dreams. Embrace the beauty and wisdom of sacred mandalas and let them guide you on your path to awakening the soul's vibration.

The Dance of Energy: Where Mandalas Meet Manifestation

Picture the universe as a grand cosmic dance floor, with energy swirling and twirling in intricate patterns. Now, imagine sacred mandalas as your personal choreographers, guiding the dance of your intentions and dreams. Just as if a conductor orchestrates a symphony, you can use mandalas to harmonize your thoughts, emotions, and desires, aligning them with the energetic frequencies of the universe. In the quantum world, you are not separated from the thing you wish to experience. You are one with the object of your desire.

Mandalas as Mirrors: Reflecting Your Deepest Desires

Imagine gazing into a mirror, seeing not only your reflection but also the vast landscapes of your aspirations. Sacred mandalas act as such mirrors, reflecting your intentions back to you, while also amplifying their resonance in the energetic web of existence. Whether your goal is to achieve career success, cultivate loving relationships, or experience vibrant health, a mandala can serve as a powerful focal point, a radiant beacon guiding your intentions toward fruition.

Example: Using Mandalas for Career Success

Let's say your goal is to flourish in your career and step into the role of leadership. You choose a mandala with vibrant reds and oranges, representing passion, confidence, and ambition. As you create the mandala, you infuse it with the intention of achieving career success.

During your meditative sessions with the mandala, you visualize yourself confidently leading meetings, making impactful decisions, and achieving your professional goals. You repeat affirmations like "I am a capable and confident leader, achieving success with ease."

Over time, you notice subtle shifts in your mindset and actions. You find yourself taking on more responsibilities, speaking up in meetings, and embracing opportunities for growth. Your energy is aligned with your intention, and the universe responds in kind, opening doors and pathways toward your desired career success.

Weaving Your Reality with Mandalas

As we journey through the realm of sacred mandalas, guided by the wisdom of Gregg Braden, we discover that these cosmic patterns are more than just intricate designs. They are portals to our intentions, bridges between our desires and the fabric of the universe. By infusing mandalas with our intentions, emotions, and positive affirmations, we weave a tapestry of transformation, where our goals manifest into reality.

Let your mandalas be your partners in positive change. Embrace the dance of energy, mirror your desires, and watch as the universe waltzes with you toward your dreams. Keep in mind the following: You are not a passive observer of the universe. You are the center of it, and your thoughts and actions create your reality.

Chapter 6

Integrating Sacred Mandalas into Daily Life

Incorporating Mandalas in Meditation and Mindfulness Practices

Incorporating Mandalas in Meditation and Mindfulness Practices

Mandalas have been used for centuries as powerful tools for healing and transformation. These sacred geometric patterns serve as a visual representation of the universe and the interconnectedness of all things.

For people in need of healing and those looking to follow their soul vibration, incorporating mandalas into meditation and mindfulness practices can be a transformative experience. These practices allow individuals to tap into the inherent healing energies of the universe and awaken their own soul's vibration.

When working with mandalas, it is essential to approach them with an open mind and heart. The intricate patterns and colors of a mandala can evoke deep emotions and connect us to our innermost selves. By gazing at a mandala during meditation, we can enter a state of deep relaxation, where the mind becomes calm, and the spirit finds solace. This state of mindfulness allows us to let go of negativity and embrace healing energy.

Incorporating mandalas into meditation and mindfulness practices can also help us develop a sense of focus and concentration. As we become absorbed in the intricate details of a mandala, our minds naturally become still, allowing us to enter a state of heightened awareness. This heightened state of consciousness enables us to connect with our inner guidance and intuition, leading us toward our soul's true path.

The journey of using sacred mandalas to heal the soul is a deeply personal one. Each individual may have a unique experience and connection with the mandalas they encounter. It is through this personal connection that the true power of mandalas is revealed. By working with mandalas consistently, individuals can unlock their own innate healing abilities and align themselves with the universal energies that surround them.

Through guided meditations, visualization exercises, and creative expression, readers will learn how to harness the transformative energies of mandalas and deepen their connection to their soul's vibration.

Whether you are seeking solace, healing, or a deeper understanding of yourself, incorporating mandalas into your meditation and mindfulness practices can be a powerful tool on your journey. The sacred mandala becomes a guide; leading you toward the realization of your true potential and helping you awaken to the vibration of your soul.

Using Mandalas for Energy Healing and Reiki

Using Mandalas for Energy Healing and Reiki

In the realm of energy healing and spiritual transformation, the power of mandalas is undeniable. These sacred geometric patterns have been used for centuries as tools for meditation, self-reflection, and healing. We will explore how using mandalas can enhance your energy-healing practices and help you tap into your soul's vibration.

To begin using mandalas for energy healing and Reiki, start by selecting a mandala that resonates with your current healing needs. Each mandala carries its own unique energy and symbolism, so trust your intuition in choosing the one that feels right for you.

Once you have your mandala, find a quiet and comfortable space where you can sit and focus your attention. Place the mandala in front of you and take a few deep breaths, allowing yourself to relax and enter a meditative state. Gaze softly at the mandala, allowing its patterns and colors to draw you in.

As you connect with the mandala, visualize the healing energy flowing through it and into your body. Feel the energy cleansing, balancing, and revitalizing your entire being. Allow any emotional or physical blockages to dissolve, making space for healing and transformation to occur.

"Unleashing Cosmic Harmony: Mandalas and Reiki Entwined in an Energetic Dance"

Picture a world where vibrant threads of energy weave a mesmerizing tapestry, guided by the gentle touch of a Reiki practitioner's hands. Now, imagine that tapestry taking the form of a dynamic mandala, a celestial masterpiece that bridges the realms of healing and artistry. It is a cosmic dance, an enchanting choreography where mandalas and Reiki merge to create a symphony of well-being.

Envision the Reiki practitioner as an energy conductor, their hands orchestrating the ebb and flow of life force energy. Now, introduce the mandala—a mystical portal pulsating with its own unique resonance. Together, they embark on a mesmerizing duet, a fusion of healing touch and sacred geometry that harmonizes the body, mind, and spirit.

The mandala's intricate patterns become pathways of energetic exploration, akin to secret passages that traverse the multidimensional landscape of existence. As the Reiki practitioner's hands traverse these pathways, a symphony of sensations unfolds—an exquisite sensory melody that resonates with the soul's deepest chords.

In this enchanting collaboration, the Reiki practitioner becomes an artist, painting strokes of energy upon the canvas of the recipient's being. Each swirl, each curve, carries an intention—a whisper that dances in tandem with the mandala's geometry. It is as if the universe itself is engaged in a grand artistic expression, an energetic ballet that transcends space and time.

The mandala, akin to a cosmic compass, guides the flow of energy with elegance and precision. It ushers the Reiki energy like a guiding star, illuminating the path to balance and restoration. As the energy ripples outward, it transforms the recipient's energetic landscape, infusing every cell with the harmonious resonance of the universe's dance.

With each gentle touch, the Reiki practitioner becomes a weaver, interlacing threads of intention and energy. The mandala, an intricate loom, transforms these threads into a tapestry of well-being, alive with hues of vitality and serenity. It is as if the very essence of existence is painted upon the canvas of the soul.

As the session culminates, the mandala's essence remains imprinted—a cosmic fingerprint etched into the recipient's energetic fabric. The dance may end, but the harmonious echoes of the mandala and Reiki continue to reverberate, a reminder of the transformative journey undertaken.

In this world where healing and creativity interlace, mandalas and Reiki forge an unbreakable bond—a cosmic duet that composes melodies of wholeness and renewal. Together, they paint a canvas of well-being, where energies converge and intentions blossom. It's a dance of cosmic proportions, a synergy of healing and art that leaves an indelible mark upon the tapestry of existence.

Creating Mandalas for Sacred Spaces and Altars

Creating Mandalas for Sacred Spaces and Altars

In the serene corners of our homes and places of worship, there exists a realm where the tangible and the spiritual converge—a space where the sacred and the mundane intertwine. This realm, often adorned with symbolic artifacts and reverent adornments, is none other than the sacred space or altar. Among the myriad forms of sacred art that can grace these sanctuaries, none is as enchanting and versatile as mandalas. Which are not just mere works of art; they are gateways to the soul.

To embark on your sacred mandala-healing journey, it is essential to understand the significance of creating mandalas for sacred spaces and altars. These spaces act as portals where we can connect with our higher selves and the spiritual energies that surround us.

To create a mandala for a sacred space or altar is to embark on a journey of alchemical transformation. The act of crafting a mandala infuses one's intentions, energy, and creativity into a symphony of form and spirit. As an artist of the soul, you wield the brush of sacred geometry, weaving threads of cosmic energy into tangible art.

Begin this alchemical process by selecting a central theme or intention for your mandala. It could be a deity, a virtue, an element of nature, or a personal affirmation. Let this intention be your guiding star, the nucleus from which the mandala's energy will radiate.

When designing a sacred space or altar, it is crucial to consider the intention and purpose behind it. Are you seeking healing, guidance, or simply a place to connect with your innermost self? Once you have identified your intention, you can begin selecting the colors, symbols, and patterns that resonate with your soul vibration.

The process of creating a sacred mandala for your space is a deeply meditative and introspective one. Begin by finding a quiet and serene environment where you can fully immerse yourself in the process. Gather materials such as colored pencils, paints, or even natural elements like flowers and leaves.

As you start designing your mandala, let your intuition guide you. There are no right or wrong choices; trust in your inner wisdom to select the colors and symbols that speak to you. Allow yourself to be present in the moment, embracing the creative flow that emerges from within.

The Palette of Symbolism: Choosing Colors and Elements

Colors, like notes in a celestial melody, possess their own vibrational frequencies and meanings. In the realm of mandalas, each hue is a brushstroke of emotion and energy. As you select the colors for your mandala, consider the resonance they hold with your intention.

For instance, red may embody passion and vitality, while green is a symbol of growth and harmony. Blue can evoke tranquility and spiritual depth, and yellow may ignite a spark of creativity and intellect. Allow the colors to sing in harmony, creating a visual symphony that resonates with your sacred space's purpose.

Elements of Nature: Infusing Life into Mandalas

Nature, with its boundless wonders, provides a rich tapestry of symbolism to infuse into your mandala. Incorporate elements such as leaves, petals, feathers, or even grains of sand. These humble offerings connect your mandala to the rhythms of the earth, reminding us of our interconnectedness with the universe.

Imagine a mandala adorning an altar with petals carefully arranged to represent the cycles of life, or a spiral evoking the energy of the cosmos. Each element becomes a vessel, carrying the essence of your intention and imbuing your sacred space with its unique magic.

Crafting Mandalas with Intention: The Creative Ritual

Creating a mandala for a sacred space is a ritual of intention, an opportunity to merge with the creative forces that shape existence. To embark on this sacred journey, set aside a tranquil space and time where you can connect with your inner self.

Begin by grounding yourself—take a few deep breaths, close your eyes, and attune to your intention. As you open your eyes, let your intuition guide your hand as you draw the central point of your mandala. From this point, patterns, shapes, and symbols flow outward like ripples in a cosmic pond.

With each line and curve, infuse your energy and intention. Let the creative process be meditation, a communion with the divine forces that dance within and around you. As you complete your mandala, feel the resonance of your intention radiating through each stroke.

An Offering of Light: Mandalas as Sacred Offerings

As your mandala graces your sacred space or altar, it becomes an offering of light—a tangible prayer that echoes your intentions into the universe. It is a bridge that links the mundane and the sacred, inviting you to connect with the higher realms.

In the soft glow of candlelight or the dappled rays of sunlight, your mandala comes to life, its intricate patterns dancing with the rhythm of cosmic energies. It becomes a conduit, channeling the intentions you have woven into its fabric, and harmonizing the energies of your sacred space.

Conclusion: A Portal of Transcendence

Creating mandalas for sacred spaces and altars is an art of transcendence—a dance between the tangible and the ethereal. It is a manifestation of intention and creativity, a symphony of colors and symbols that speak the language of the soul.

As you embark on this artistic journey, remember that your mandala is not merely an object—it is a portal. It is a portal through which you can transcend the boundaries of the physical and venture into the realms of the sacred. Let each stroke of your brush be a step into the cosmic dance, a movement in the grand choreography of existence.

In the presence of your mandala, time seems to bend, and the boundaries between the ordinary and the divine blur. It becomes a mirror that reflects your inner landscapes, your dreams, and your aspirations. Just as a prism refracts light into a spectrum of colors, your mandala refracts your intentions and emotions into a kaleidoscope of energy.

As you gaze upon your creation within the sanctuary of your sacred space, you become the observer and the observed, the creator and the creation. The mandala becomes a vessel for your soul's expression, an invitation to explore the depths of your being and the expanses of the universe.

In this sacred partnership between artist and art, intention, and manifestation, you weave a tapestry of energy that resonates far beyond the physical realm. Your mandala becomes a beacon of light, radiating your intentions into the cosmos and drawing to you the energies that mirror your own.

And so, dear seeker of the sacred, as you embark on the journey of creating mandalas for your sacred spaces and altars, remember that you are a cosmic weaver, a bridge between the seen and the unseen. With each stroke of your brush, you infuse your intentions into the fabric of reality, contributing your unique thread to the tapestry of existence.

Your mandala becomes a portal, a threshold through which you can step into a realm of higher consciousness, a space where the ordinary transforms into the extraordinary. It is a testament to your creative power, a mirror that reflects your inner world, and a bridge that connects you to the energies of the universe.

So, let your mandalas be a symphony of colors, a dance of shapes, and a fusion of intention and artistry. Let them be your silent prayers, your cosmic offerings, and your portals of transcendence. As you craft each mandala with love, intention, and creativity, you unlock the door to a realm where the sacred and the mundane embrace in a harmonious dance of energy, forever changing the landscapes of your heart and soul.

And as you stand in the presence of your mandala-adorned sacred space, you may just catch a glimpse of the cosmic dance, where the rhythm of creation pulses through every fiber of your being, and the symphony of existence unfolds in the colors and patterns of your sacred art.

Chapter 7

Sharing the Healing Power of Mandalas

Facilitating Mandala Workshops and Group Healing Sessions

Facilitating Mandala Workshops and Group Healing Sessions

The Magic of Mandalas Unveiled

In the realm of healing and self-discovery, few tools are as versatile and potent as the mandala. A symphony of shapes and colors, a mandala has the remarkable ability to resonate with the depths of our being, offering solace, insight, and transformation. Now, imagine harnessing this transformative power within the embrace of a group setting. Welcome to the world of facilitating mandala workshops and group healing sessions—a sacred space where individual journeys merge, energies interweave, and healing ripples through the collective.

Creating a sacred environment is crucial when conducting mandala workshops or group healing sessions. Begin by selecting a tranquil and harmonious setting that fosters a sense of peace and serenity. This could be a cozy studio, a natural outdoor space, or any place that resonates with the energy of healing and transformation. Set up the space with soft lighting, calming music, and natural elements like crystals, flowers, or incense to enhance the ambiance.

In a workshop or healing session, the mandala serves as a common ground, a unifying force that bridges the gap between diverse individuals. It invites participants to immerse themselves in a creative process that transcends verbal language, allowing for deep introspection and cathartic release. The mandala becomes a canvas upon which stories, emotions, and intentions are woven, creating a tapestry of shared experience.

Weaving the Tapestry of Connection

Imagine a room bathed in soft, ambient light, with eager hearts and curious minds, gathered around a table adorned with an array of art supplies. Each participant holds a blank canvas, a metaphor for the uncharted territory of their inner world. As the journey unfolds, the facilitator guides the group through a series of meditative exercises, inviting them to connect with their intentions, emotions, and the energy of the collective.

With gentle guidance, participants embark on their mandala creation, letting their intuition and creativity flow freely. The room becomes a sanctuary, where vulnerability is honored, and judgment dissolves. As the mandalas take shape, a sense of interconnectedness emerges—a tapestry woven from individual threads of expression, forming a harmonious whole.

Harmonizing Energies, Sharing Insights

In the sacred space of a mandala workshop, energies harmonize, and stories intertwine. Participants may find themselves drawn to certain colors, symbols, or patterns, each holding a unique resonance. As the mandalas evolve, they become vessels of insight, reflecting the inner landscapes of each creator.

In a group setting, the insights gained from one participant's mandala can ripple through the collective, inspiring a sense of resonance and recognition. Themes emerge, and universal truths are unveiled, fostering a sense of unity and shared experience. As participants share their creations and insights, the room is filled with a chorus of understanding, empathy, and healing.

Navigating Transformation and Healing

As the workshop or group session unfolds, a powerful transformation takes place—both individually and collectively. The act of creating a mandala becomes an act of empowerment, a declaration of one's own unique voice and journey. Through the process, participants may uncover buried emotions, release stagnant energy, and gain clarity on unresolved issues.

The healing power of the mandala is amplified within the collective energy of a group. As participants share their stories and vulnerabilities, a safe container is formed, allowing for deep healing to occur. Through the act of creation and sharing, wounds are acknowledged, compassion is cultivated, and a sense of release is experienced.

Experiencing the Alchemy of Group Energy

In the alchemical crucible of a mandala workshop, something profound transpires—the melding of individual energies to create a potent elixir of healing and transformation. The group becomes a living, breathing organism, an interconnected web of souls, each contributing to the collective tapestry of growth.

Participants often leave these sessions with a heightened sense of self-awareness, empowerment, and connection. The mandalas created during the workshop become tangible symbols of their journey, serving as reminders of the insights gained and the healing achieved. The group dynamic amplifies the healing potential, creating a ripple effect that extends beyond the workshop space and into daily life.

Guiding the Mandala Dance: The Role of the Facilitator

As a facilitator, it is essential to establish clear intentions and guidelines for the workshop or healing session and to create a safe and sacred container for participants to explore their inner landscapes. Encourage participants to approach the mandala work with an open mind and heart, emphasizing the non-judgmental nature of the process. Create a safe space where individuals feel comfortable expressing their emotions, sharing their stories, and embracing vulnerability. Encourage active listening and respectful communication among participants, fostering a supportive and compassionate atmosphere.

Begin the workshop by introducing the concept of sacred mandalas and their significance in healing and transformation. Explain how mandalas can serve as powerful tools for self-discovery, self-expression, and healing. Share examples of different mandala designs and their symbolic meanings, allowing participants to connect with the energy that resonates with them. Provide a variety of art supplies, such as colored pencils, paints, and markers, allowing individuals to choose their preferred medium for their mandala creation.

Through guided meditations, reflective prompts, and gentle encouragement, the facilitator invites participants to journey within and express their unique essence on the canvas. They hold space for vulnerability, witnessing each participant's process with reverence and non-judgment.

Guide participants through visualization exercises to help them connect with their inner selves and tap into their soul's vibrations. Encourage them to explore their emotions, thoughts, and memories as they embark on their mandala journey. Support them in understanding that there is no right or wrong way to create a mandala; it is a personal and intuitive process.

Throughout the workshop or healing session, offer guidance and support, but also allow individuals the freedom to express themselves authentically. Encourage participants to share their experiences and insights, fostering a sense of community and connection. Facilitate discussions on the symbolism and meaning behind their mandalas, helping them gain further clarity and understanding of their healing journey.

The facilitator also weaves the threads of connection, fostering an environment of trust and authenticity. They skillfully navigate the group dynamics, ensuring that each voice is heard, and each journey is honored. With intuitive guidance, the facilitator helps participants navigate any emotional or energetic shifts that may arise, ensuring that the experience is one of healing and growth.

Creating Sacred Spaces for Transformation

In the tapestry of life, mandala workshops and group healing sessions are like sacred gatherings, where souls converge to weave their stories, energies, and intentions. The act of creating mandalas within a group setting amplifies the healing potential, inviting participants to embark on a shared journey of self-discovery and transformation.

As participants leave the workshop or session, they carry with them the vibrational imprints of the collective experience—the shared laughter, tears, insights, and connections. The mandalas created during these sessions become portals, anchoring the energies of healing and development, and serving as potent reminders of the transformative power that lies within each of us.

So, whether you find yourself participating in a mandala workshop or facilitating one, remember that you are a weaver of energies, a guide in the realm of self-exploration, and a catalyst for collective healing. Through the harmonious dance of group energy and the transformative artistry of mandalas, we co-create spaces of profound connection, authenticity, and growth.

Using Mandalas in Therapy and Counseling

Using Mandalas in Therapy and Counseling

The therapeutic use of mandalas stems from the understanding that they represent the interconnectedness of the universe and reflect the wholeness within everyone. By engaging with mandalas, individuals can access their subconscious mind, release emotional blockages, and gain insight into their innermost thoughts and feelings. These intricate patterns act as a visual representation of the individual's psyche, providing a gateway to self-discovery and healing.

One of the primary benefits of using mandalas in therapy is their ability to induce a state of relaxation and calmness. As individuals color or create mandalas, they enter a meditative state, which activates the parasympathetic nervous system, promoting a sense of peace and well-being. This state of relaxation allows for a deeper exploration of one's emotions and thoughts, empowering individuals to confront and heal past traumas or emotional wounds.

Moreover, mandalas serve as a non-verbal form of expression, making them particularly useful in therapy settings where individuals struggle with verbal communication. Regardless of one's artistic abilities, anyone can engage with mandalas, allowing for a form of self-expression that transcends language barriers. Through the process of creating or coloring mandalas, individuals can access their subconscious mind, expressing their deepest emotions and thoughts in a safe and non-judgmental space.

Furthermore, mandalas can act as a guide for personal transformation. As individuals engage with these sacred patterns, they can set intentions for their healing journey, manifesting their desires, and focusing their energy on positive change. The act of creating or coloring mandalas becomes a sacred ritual, allowing individuals to align with their soul's vibration, connect with their higher selves, and access their innate wisdom.

Healing with Mandalas: The Power of Art Therapy

Through the interpretation of a mandala, individuals can gain insight into their emotions, thoughts, and behaviors, as well as their inner strengths and resources. It can be a powerful tool for self-discovery, healing, and personal growth.

Imagine yourself sitting in front of a mandala, taking in all its intricate details and vibrant colors. As you observe the shapes and patterns within the design, you may notice a stirring within you - a tug at your emotions, a shift in your energy, or a flood of memories.

This is where the magic of interpretation begins. By paying attention to these inner experiences, you can begin to unravel the meaning behind the mandala and what it is trying to communicate to you.

Colors, shapes, and patterns can all hold significant symbolic meaning, and it's important to remain open and curious as you explore what they evoke in you. Perhaps the color blue fills you with a sense of calm and peace, while the shape of a circle speaks to your sense of wholeness and completeness.

I have seen the transformative power of mandalas in helping individuals connect with their inner selves and work through emotional and psychological issues. Mandalas, with their intricate designs and sacred geometry, have been used for centuries in various spiritual and cultural traditions as a tool for meditation and self-discovery.

For example, one client I worked with created a mandala with a lot of dark colors and sharp angles. As we explored the meaning behind her creation, she revealed that she was feeling depressed and anxious about a recent breakup. The sharp angles represented her feelings of anger and frustration, while the dark colors represented her sadness and grief. Through the process of creating the mandala and exploring its meaning, she was able to release her emotions and gain clarity about her situation.

Another client I worked with created a mandala with a lot of circular shapes and vibrant colors. As we explored the meaning behind her creation, she revealed that she was feeling a sense of joy and abundance in her life. The circular shapes represented her connection to the universe and her sense of wholeness, while the vibrant colors represented her energy and vitality.

Through mandala art therapy, clients can gain insight into their emotions, thoughts, and behaviors, as well as their inner strengths and resources. It can be a powerful tool for self-discovery, healing, and personal growth. By creating a mandala, you are creating a portrait of yourself in the moment, expressing your inner self through color and shape. So, let your instincts and feelings guide you as you embark on your own mandala art therapy journey.

In art therapy, the process of creating a mandala can be just as important as the final product. It is a chance for the individual to tap into their intuition and creativity, allowing their inner world to be expressed in a visual form. As they work through the design, they may uncover insights and revelations about their own emotions, thoughts, and behaviors.

One technique I often use is to encourage clients to create mandalas that represent specific themes or aspects of their lives, such as their relationships, self-esteem, or goals. By doing so, they can explore and work through these areas in a safe and supportive space. For example, if someone is struggling with feelings of anxiety, they may create a mandala that focuses on the theme of calm and balance.

The interpretation of the mandala can also be a powerful tool for self-discovery. By examining the shapes, colors, and patterns within the mandala, clients can gain insight into their own inner workings and gain a greater understanding of themselves. For example, they may notice that certain colors or shapes evoke specific emotions or memories, which can then be explored further in therapy.

It is important to remember that there is no right or wrong interpretation of a mandala. Rather, the interpretation should be guided by the individual's personal experiences, emotions, and intuition. An art therapist may ask open-ended questions or provide prompts to help the individual explore their mandala more deeply and gain a greater understanding of themselves and their inner world.

As you delve deeper into your experience with the mandala, you may find it helpful to journal your thoughts and emotions, allowing yourself to freely express whatever comes up for you. This can help you gain clarity and insight into the underlying themes and messages of the mandala.

As you dive more into your mandala, you may find yourself uncovering a wealth of information about your inner world. Pay attention to the feelings, memories, and sensations that come up for you as you explore the design. What emotions do certain colors evoke? What memories or associations come up with shapes or symbols? Allow yourself to be curious and open-minded as you delve into the meaning behind your mandala.

What if negative emotions appear?

Negative emotions can often arise during the creation of a mandala. This is perfectly normal and should not be suppressed or ignored. Instead, we should embrace these emotions and allow them to flow through us, expressing them in our mandala art therapy and approaching them with compassion and non-judgment. Acknowledge and accept the emotions that arise without trying to push them away or suppress them. Remember that these emotions are a natural and normal part of the human experience.

Once you have acknowledged the negative emotions, consider how you can express and release them through your mandala. Maybe you choose to use darker colors or sharper lines to represent your emotions, or maybe you decide to incorporate symbols or imagery that represent the source of your emotions.

As you continue to work on your mandala, you may find that the negative emotions start to dissipate and shift into a more positive or neutral state. This is a natural and normal part of the healing process.

Think of your negative emotions as a visitor who has come to your inner world. It is important to acknowledge their presence, give them a voice, and allow them to be expressed through your mandala. You may choose to use darker colors or sharp, angular lines to represent these emotions.

But don't stop there. Once you have expressed your negative emotions through your mandala, it is time to release them. You can do this by intentionally letting go of the emotions and surrendering them to the universe, trusting that they will be transformed into something positive.

You can also add symbols of healing and transformation to your mandala, such as a lotus flower or a spiral, to represent the journey from darkness to light or a spirit animal that you can identify with.

Remember, your mandala art therapy is a safe and sacred space for you to explore your inner world and release any negative emotions that may be holding you back. Trust in the process and know that you have the power to transform even the darkest of emotions into something beautiful and empowering.

One of the magical things about interpreting a mandala is the insight it can provide into your own psyche. You may discover parts of yourself that you didn't even know existed or gain a deeper understanding of your emotions, thoughts, and behaviors. By tapping into your inner strengths and resources, you can use this newfound knowledge to promote personal growth and healing.

Remember that the goal of using mandalas in art therapy is not to erase or eliminate negative emotions, but rather to provide a safe and creative outlet for expressing and processing them. Through the process of creating and interpreting your mandala, you can gain insight and understanding into your emotions and inner world, and ultimately, find a sense of healing and growth.

So, embrace your negative emotions with love and compassion, and let your mandala be a tool for release and transformation. So, free yourself and dive into the mysterious world of mandalas. Remember, there are no right or wrong answers - only a vast, endless landscape of possibilities to explore and know yourself on a deeper level.

Spreading Awareness and Inspiring Others through Mandalas

Spreading Awareness and Inspiring Others through Mandalas

For those in need of healing, following their soul vibration, mandalas offer a profound journey of self-discovery and transformation. As individuals navigate the intricate designs of a sacred mandala, they are invited to delve deep within themselves, connecting with their innermost desires, fears, and dreams. The process of coloring or creating a mandala can be a meditative practice, allowing one to quiet the mind and tap into the wisdom of the soul. By engaging with these sacred symbols, individuals can release emotional blockages, find solace in their pain, and ultimately experience a profound sense of healing and wholeness.

But the power of mandalas extends beyond personal healing. They can touch the hearts and souls of others, spreading awareness and inspiring a collective awakening. Using mandalas, we can communicate our deepest truths and share our experiences of healing and transformation. Whether it be through exhibiting our own mandala creations, hosting workshops, or even just sharing our stories, we can inspire others to embark on their own sacred mandala journeys. By doing so, we contribute to a collective healing movement, igniting a ripple effect of positive change in the world.

In a world brimming with noise and distractions, the simple act of creation can become a powerful tool for sparking awareness and inspiring change. Among the myriad forms of artistic expression, the mandala stands as a unique and enchanting medium—a symphony of shapes and colors that has the remarkable ability to captivate hearts, awaken minds, and ignite transformation. As we embark on a journey through the captivating realm of mandalas, let us explore how these intricate circles of art can serve as beacons of awareness, vehicles of inspiration, and catalysts for positive change.

The Mandala: A Universal Language of Visual Poetry

Imagine gazing upon a mandala—its intricate patterns spiraling outward like a cosmic dance, its vibrant hues whispering ancient secrets, its symmetrical geometry inviting you to explore its depths. It is a language of visual poetry, transcending cultural boundaries, spoken words, and written scripts. Within the sacred embrace of a mandala, one can find a respite from the chaos of the external world, a portal to the sanctum of the soul, and a canvas upon which intentions, emotions, and stories are woven.

The universality of the mandala renders it a potent vessel for spreading awareness. Like a drop of vibrant ink falling into a still pond, the creation of a mandala ripples outwards, reaching souls near and far. Its symbolism is not confined by language barriers; rather, it speaks to the heart, resonating with the innate wisdom that resides within us all.

Empowering Voices, Igniting Conversations

A single mandala has the power to kindle conversations, catalyzing discussions on a myriad of topics. When an artist chooses to infuse their creation with a message, an intention, or a cause, the mandala becomes a vibrant tapestry of storytelling. Take, for instance, an artist who crafts a mandala adorned with symbols of environmental harmony—a lush forest, flowing rivers, and vibrant wildlife. This creation becomes a silent advocate for Mother Earth, urging viewers to pause and contemplate their role as stewards of the planet. As others engage with the mandala, it becomes a catalyst for dialogue, inviting questions, reflections, and collective action.

Spreading Awareness through Mandala Campaigns

In our digital age, the mandala has ventured beyond canvases and paper, finding new homes in virtual realms. Social media platforms have become vibrant canvases where artists, activists, and individuals alike converge to share their mandalas and their messages. Enter the realm of mandala campaigns—an innovative way to unite people, inspire change, and create a ripple effect of awareness.

Imagine a global movement where artists from all corners of the world unite under the banner of a common cause. Each artist creates a mandala that encapsulates their unique perspective and passion for change. These mandalas flood social media feeds, radiating their messages of hope, unity, and transformation. As the campaign gains momentum, conversations ensue, minds are expanded, and seeds of change are sown. The mandala becomes a silent messenger, traversing borders and transcending boundaries, carrying with it a harmonious symphony of voices united in purpose.

Cultivating Mindfulness and Inner Transformation

Beyond its role as a vehicle for spreading awareness, the mandala has the power to inspire profound inner transformation. Engaging with the creation or contemplation of a mandala invites us to step into the present moment, cultivating mindfulness and connecting with the essence of our being. As we immerse ourselves in the creative process, worries of the past and anxieties of the future dissipate, leaving us attuned to the symphony of colors, shapes, and energies before us.

This state of mindfulness creates a fertile ground for introspection, self-awareness, and personal growth. Like a mirror held up to the soul, the mandala reflects our inner landscapes, illuminating aspects of ourselves that may have remained hidden. As we observe the choices we make while crafting a mandala, the colors we select, and the symbols we incorporate, we gain insights into our emotions, desires, and intentions.

Closing Thoughts: Mandalas as Catalysts for Change

In a world that thirsts for awareness, connection, and positive transformation, the mandala emerges as a luminous beacon—a symbol of unity, creativity, and limitless potential. As artists, activists, and individuals, we hold within us the power to create mandalas that transcend mere aesthetics and become agents of change. Through our intentions, messages, and stories, we can infuse these intricate circles with the energy of transformation, inspiring others to awaken, reflect, and embark on their own journeys of awareness.

As the kaleidoscope of a mandala turns, may we remember that each vibrant fragment contributes to the whole—a symphony of colors, shapes, and energies that echo the harmonious dance of life itself. Let us, then, step onto the canvas of our world, wielding the brush of creativity and the palette of intention, and paint mandalas that ignite awareness, kindle inspiration, and illuminate the path to a brighter future.

Chapter 8

Nurturing the Soul's Vibration

Self-Care Practices to Enhance Soul Connection

Self-Care Practices to Enhance Soul Connection

In the sacred journey of healing and transformation, connecting with your soul's vibration is vital. It is through this deep connection that you can experience inner peace, profound healing, and a sense of purpose. By embracing self-care practices that enhance this soul connection, you can embark on a transformative journey of self-discovery and healing. In this subchapter, we will explore various self-care practices that can help you tap into the power of sacred mandalas for healing and aligning with your soul's vibration.

1. Meditation and Mindfulness: Begin your day with a quiet meditation practice to center yourself and connect with your inner being. Allow the stillness to guide you towards a deep soul connection, where you can listen to the whispers of your soul's desires. Practice mindfulness throughout the day, bringing your attention to

the present moment and nurturing a deeper understanding of your true self.
2. Journaling and Reflection: Set aside time each day to journal your thoughts, feelings, and experiences. This practice encourages self-reflection and helps you gain clarity about your emotions and desires. Use your journal as a tool for self-discovery, exploring your dreams, and setting intentions that align with your soul's vibration.
3. Nature Immersion: Spend time in nature, allowing its beauty and serenity to nourish your soul. Take walks in the woods, sit by the ocean, or simply spend time in your garden. Nature has a way of grounding us and connecting us to something greater than ourselves, enabling a deeper connection with our soul's vibration.
4. Creative Expression: Engage in creative activities that resonate with your soul. Whether it's painting, writing, dancing, or playing music, find an outlet that allows you to express yourself authentically. The act of creation is a powerful tool for connecting with your innermost self and aligning with your soul's vibration.
5. Sacred Mandala Rituals: Incorporate sacred mandalas into your self-care routine. These intricate geometric designs are powerful tools for healing and transformation. Engage in mandala coloring, meditation, or creation to deepen your connection with your soul's vibration and experience profound healing.

Remember, self-care is not selfish; it is an essential part of your healing journey. By incorporating these practices into your daily life, you can cultivate a deeper connection with your soul and align with your truest desires. Embrace the power of sacred mandalas and embark on a transformative journey of healing and self-discovery. Awaken your soul's vibration and experience the profound joy and peace that comes from living in alignment with your true self.

Maintaining Balance and Harmony through Mandalas

Maintaining Balance and Harmony through Mandalas

In our fast-paced and chaotic world, finding balance and harmony can seem like an elusive goal. We often find ourselves caught up in the hustle and bustle of daily life, feeling disconnected from our true selves and searching for a sense of peace and well-being. Thankfully, there is a powerful tool that can guide us on this healing journey – sacred mandalas.

One of the most beautiful aspects of sacred mandalas is their ability to connect us with our soul vibration. Every individual has a unique energy signature, a soul vibration that is as distinct as a fingerprint. However, due to the demands and pressures of modern life, we often lose touch with our authentic selves. Mandalas provide a pathway for us to rediscover and align with our soul's vibration.

When we immerse ourselves in the creation or contemplation of a mandala, we enter a state of deep relaxation and mindfulness. This allows us to quiet the mind, release stress and tension, and open ourselves up to the wisdom and guidance of our higher self. Through this process, we can strengthen our connection to our soul vibration, gaining clarity and insight into our true desires and purpose.

Moreover, working with sacred mandalas can also help us heal on a physical, emotional, and spiritual level. The symmetrical and harmonious nature of mandalas brings a sense of order and coherence to our energy field. They can help us release energetic blockages, restore flow, and promote healing and well-being. By engaging with mandalas regularly, we can create a sacred space within ourselves, where healing and transformation can take place.

Whether you are seeking solace from emotional pain, physical ailments, or simply a desire to connect with your inner self, the journey of sacred mandalas offers a profound and transformative experience. It is an invitation to slow down, listen to your soul's whispers, and embrace the beauty and harmony that resides within you...

Are you ready to embark on this transformative journey? Let the sacred mandalas guide you back to your true self, restoring balance, and harmony to your life. Open your heart, embrace the beauty of the mandala, and allow it to awaken your soul's vibration.

Continuing the Healing Journey with Sacred Mandalas

Continuing the Healing Journey with Sacred Mandalas

In our journey toward healing and self-discovery, sacred mandalas serve as powerful tools to guide us along the path of transformation. These intricate geometric designs have been used for centuries by various cultures as a means of connecting with the divine and accessing the healing energy within us. In this subchapter, we will delve deeper into the profound impact that sacred mandalas can have on our healing journey, and how they can help us align with our soul's vibration.

For those in need of healing, the sacred mandala becomes a sacred portal through which we can access our innermost being. As we immerse ourselves in the vibrant colors and intricate patterns, we can quiet the mind and enter a state of deep relaxation. This state of stillness creates the perfect environment for healing to occur, as it allows us to release any emotional or physical imbalances that may be blocking our well-being.

Following our soul's vibration is an essential aspect of our healing journey. Each of us has a unique energetic signature, a soul vibration that is specific to us. By working with sacred mandalas, we can attune ourselves to this vibration and align with our true essence. As we connect with the mandala's energy, we begin to resonate with its healing frequencies, allowing us to tap into our innate wisdom and intuition.

The sacred mandala is not only a tool for healing; it is also a mirror that reflects to us our own inner landscape. As we engage with these intricate designs, we may notice certain emotions or memories surfacing. This reflection allows us to explore and process these experiences, facilitating our healing on a deeper level. By embracing what arises within us while working with the mandala, we can release any stagnant energy and make space for new growth and transformation.

Moreover, the sacred mandala acts as a guide on our healing journey, offering us insights and guidance along the way. Each mandala has its own unique symbolism and energy, which can be interpreted and understood through meditation and contemplation. By allowing ourselves to be receptive to the messages of the mandala, we open ourselves to new perspectives and possibilities.

Conclusion

Embracing the Soul's Vibration through Sacred Mandalas

Conclusion: Embracing the Soul's Vibration through Sacred Mandalas In our journey towards healing and transformation, sacred mandalas have emerged as powerful tools for connecting with our soul's vibration. These intricate geometric designs hold the key to unlocking our innermost desires, guiding us toward a path of self-discovery and spiritual growth. For those in need of healing and yearning to follow their soul's vibration, the sacred mandala becomes a transformative journey that offers solace, inspiration, and profound insight.

Throughout this book, "Awakening the Soul's Vibration: Sacred Mandalas for Healing and Transformation," we have explored the profound connection between the soul and these sacred symbols. We have delved into the history and significance of mandalas, uncovering their roots in ancient cultures and their role as gateways to the divine. Now, as we reach the conclusion of our exploration, we must embrace the transformative power of these sacred mandalas and allow them to guide us on our healing journey.

The healing properties of sacred mandalas lie in their ability to harmonize our mind, body, and spirit. As we immerse ourselves in their intricate patterns, we activate dormant energies within us, igniting a process of self-healing and transformation. The soul's vibration resonates with the mandala's energy, creating a synergy that brings forth profound healing and alignment.

By embracing the sacred mandala as a healing journey for the soul, we open ourselves up to a world of possibilities. Through the practice of coloring or meditating with mandalas, we enter a state of deep relaxation and mindfulness, allowing us to release emotional blockages and restore balance within ourselves. The vibrational frequencies of the mandala connect us to higher realms of consciousness, where we can tap into our intuition, gain clarity, and find purpose.

Furthermore, the sacred mandala serves as a mirror, reflecting the essence of our soul back to us. As we engage with these spiritual symbols, we uncover hidden aspects of ourselves, revealing our true nature and potential. The process of self-discovery and self-acceptance becomes an integral part of our healing journey, as we recognize and embrace the unique vibration of our soul.

In conclusion, for those in need of healing and seeking to follow their soul's vibration, the sacred mandala provides a profound and transformative experience. By immersing ourselves in the intricate patterns and vibrant colors, we tap into the ancient wisdom embedded within these sacred symbols. Through the practice of coloring, meditating, and engaging with mandalas, we awaken our soul's vibration, restoring balance, and finding our true selves. May this journey through sacred mandalas guide you toward healing, transformation, and a deeper connection with your soul's essence.

Testimonials on Custom Mandalas by MurielXpression

The Awakening Orchid (Tokyo, Japan)

"I was feeling lost and disconnected, searching for something to anchor me. Then I discovered the captivating mandala created by Muriel. As I immersed myself in its geometrical patterns, I felt a surge of energy, like an orchid blooming in my soul. It awakened my inner strength and helped me find my purpose. Now, I navigate life's challenges with grace and resilience."

The Serene Seascape (Sydney, Australia)

"Living in a bustling city, stress had become an unwelcome companion in my life. Yearning for peace and serenity, I stumbled upon the mesmerizing mandala art of MurielXpression. The tranquil colors and gentle curves of the mandala transported me to a serene seascape. With each breath, I felt the waves of calm washing over me, leaving behind anxiety and worry. This enchanting artwork has become my daily retreat to find inner peace."

The Soulful Symphony (New Orleans, USA)

"I had been searching for a way to reconnect with my true essence, longing to hear the symphony of my soul once again. The moment I laid eyes on the captivating mandala masterpiece created by Muriel, my heart skipped a beat. As I focused on the vibrant colors and intricate design, it was as if my soul had found its voice. The melody of my being resonated through every stroke, leaving me feeling alive, empowered, and deeply connected to my purpose."

The Blissful Blooms (Paris, France)

"Amidst my chaotic city life, I was yearning for a sense of beauty and joy. The mandala I received from Muriel became a beacon of bliss in my life. Each petal seemed to whisper stories of growth, resilience, and blossoming into one's true potential. The energy of the mandala nurtured my spirit, filling my days with gratitude, wonder, and a renewed appreciation for the simple joys of life."

The Resilient Phoenix (Edinburgh, Scotland)

"Nestled amidst the captivating beauty of Edinburgh, I found myself on a journey of personal transformation and growth. My mandala created by Muriel, adorned with luminous colors, resonated deeply with my spirit. As I delved into its mesmerizing depths, I felt a surge of resilience and strength rising within me, like a phoenix soaring above life's challenges. The mandala became a symbol of my own inner power and a reminder of my ability to rise from the ashes of adversity. It has become an integral part of my daily practice, igniting my spirit and empowering me to embrace life's journey with unwavering courage."

The Radiant Revival (Hawaii, USA)

"After a period of emotional turmoil, I longed for a revival of my being and a rekindling of my inner light. The unique mandala, glowing with vivid colors, captured my attention like a beacon of hope. As I gazed into its depths, I felt a surge of healing energy enveloping me. The mandala awakened dormant dreams, reigniting my passion and reminding me of the infinite possibilities that lie within. I am forever grateful for this radiant revival. Thank you, Muriel, for designing it for me."

The Tranquil Oasis (Belize, Central America)

"Living amidst the serene beauty of Belize, I sought a sanctuary that would deepen my connection with nature and my own inner stillness. The mandala, inspired by the island's tranquility, became my sacred oasis. Its gentle swirls and soothing shades transported me to a realm of profound calmness and inner peace. This captivating artwork has become my daily ritual, reminding me to embrace the serenity within. Forever grateful to MurielXpression"

The Sacred Tapestry (Cairo, Egypt)

"In the mystical land of ancient traditions, I yearned for a connection to the sacred threads that weave through all existence. The mandala I received from Muriel, is a tapestry of spiritual symbols and cosmic energies, which captured my soul. As I meditated on the design, I felt a deep sense of unity and reverence for the divine. This mandala has become my sacred portal, guiding me on a transformative journey of self-discovery and spiritual awakening."

The Transcendent Dance Location: Prague, Czech Republic

"In the heart of Prague, I found myself longing for a means to transcend the boundaries of the mundane and tap into the realm of the extraordinary. The renowned healer's mandala, an enchanting dance of colors and shapes, beckoned me toward transcendence. As I immersed myself in its vibrant energy, I felt my spirit soar and my consciousness expand. This captivating artwork has become my portal to infinite possibilities, inspiring me to live a life beyond limitations."

These unique testimonials from around the world offer a glimpse into the transformative power of the mandalas created by MurielXpression. Each individual shares a personal journey of healing, self-discovery, and empowerment, inspired by the captivating energy and symbolism embedded within these sacred artworks. Experience the magic for yourself and unlock the hidden potential within. Order your mandala today and embark on your own extraordinary journey of growth and transformation.

Printed in the USA
CPSIA information can be obtained
at www.ICGtesting.com
JSHW071623191023
50462JS00003B/28